Sam the SUPERSTAR Puppy

By
Lorna Jackson

Published by Wee Star

Copyright © Lorna Jackson 2024

The right of Lorna Jackson to be identified as the author of this work has been asserted in accordance with the Copyright, Designs and Patent Act, 1988

Cover Artwork and Illustrations
© Mandy Sinclair

Map illustration By Lorna Jackson

This is a work of fiction. All the names, characters, businesses, events and incidents in this book are the product of the author's imagination. Any resemblance to actual persons, living or dead, or actual events is purely coincidental.

Dedicated

To All Children Who Love Dogs

Chapter 1
Christmas Surprises

Sophie tiptoed past Grandpa, who was snoring quietly in his chair, to reach the window. She watched the snow swirling and falling gently on the ground and put her hand onto her jumper to settle the butterflies dancing inside her tummy. Darkness was beginning to fall and the street looked like fairyland with twinkling lights hanging from roofs and garages all along her street, golden reindeers glistening as they stood guarding Victoria's garden next door. Christmas lights were magical thought Sophie.

She hoped Mum and Dad would be home soon – it was Christmas Eve and she wondered what was keeping them. Hearing her brothers arguing, she tiptoed over to them. 'You two need to play quietly and not wake Gran and Grandpa.'

she whispered.

'Sophie, I'm really bored. I want to have some fun,' whispered Harry. 'I'm going out to play in the snow. I'm going to build a snowman for Santa to see!' he said, hopping from foot to foot.

Sophie, who knew that Harry's complaints would just get louder, agreed. 'Okay, we can go out for a little while. Let's see if there's enough snow to make a snowman.'

Sophie was ten and felt so much more grown up than Harry who was only six. Although her other brother, Max, was eight, he often had his nose in a book and wasn't much help! The idea of a snowman was enough to get his interest though and he followed Sophie and Harry into the garden. It was cold outside and the air was frosty.

'Watch this,' said Max as he breathed out, his breath stretching in front of him.

'I can do that too,' said Harry, joining in.

'Oh look, Santa will be able to see the way

to the houses with all these stars and that big moon,' said Max, staring up at the sky.

'I hope he remembers I want some new Lego,' muttered Harry. Sophie laughed.

Max pointed. 'Look – a shooting star!'

They stopped to look up into the night sky. Sure enough, a star seemed to glide across the sky and stop in a place all of its own and then begin to fade, leaving a wispy trail.

'I read in a book that if you see a shooting star you can make a wish,' said Max.

'Really?' said Sophie. 'But making a wish doesn't mean it'll come true.'

'Maybe not, but if you believe it might,' he said.

Sophie watched as Max and Harry rolled a very small head for their snowman. She stared up at the shooting star, now fading fast in the sky, and wondered if she should make a wish. Would it come true if she did? She closed her eyes and lifted her head towards the sky and, in a little whisper so that Max and Harry didn't hear, made her wish: 'I wish I could have a puppy to play with, to love and that would love me back.' She kept her eyes closed tightly and hoped.

'Oh Harry, you numpty!' shouted Max, bringing Sophie back to reality. She looked over at Max who was not at all pleased with Harry – he had dropped the little snowman's head on the ground and now it was all smashed.

'Don't worry Harry, it's just snow. We can easily put it back together,' Sophie said as she began to mould the head back into shape, looking straight at Max.

'I'll get stones for his eyes,' said Harry. 'I can see two black ones beside the fence.'

'Good idea,' said Max. He was happy to keep Harry away from the snowman. 'See if you can find a short stick for his nose.'

Harry thought that was a daft idea and he

disappeared into the kitchen. A minute later, he ran back out. 'Max, Max,' he shouted. 'Look – this'll be much better, it will glow in the dark for Santa!'

'Great idea Harry,' said Sophie and Max laughed. 'Snowmen don't usually have a satsuma for a nose, but it's the right colour.'

Harry came running up the garden towards the snowman, ready to stick on his nose. Two voices rang out in the darkness,

'Careful Harry!'

'Take your time and be gentle,' guided Sophie.

Sophie and Max watched Harry walk with large, slow steps towards the snowman and very carefully place the satsuma on his face. As Max put a hat and a scarf on him, Sophie thought it was a good snowman – not very tall, but quite smart.

She looked up at the sky one last time as they all headed to the back door. She knew her wish would not come true because Dad had said no to a puppy lots of times. They were too much work. She sighed. When I am grown up, she thought, I will buy a dog of my own.

She saw Gran at the back door, smiling. 'What a lovely snowman, he's quite little but quite perfect,' she said.

'The satsuma's my idea,' said Harry.

'Good choice,' said Gran. 'Now let's have some dinner before Mum and Dad come back. They've had a very busy day,' she said as she smiled at Grandpa who had woken up and come to see their snowman.

As Sophie had passed the snowman, she was sure it had winked at her. She looked back one last time before heading into the house, but no winks this time. How strange!

Sophie, Harry and Max all hurried in. The smell of Gran's dinner, a familiar warm cheesy smell, was floating into the back garden and making Sophie feel a bit hungry. Building a snowman with her brothers was hard work.

'We saw a shooting star,' said Harry through a mouthful of dinner. 'Max said you can make a wish, so I wished that Santa'll bring me a gigantic box of Lego.'

'Maybe gigantic is a bit too much?' suggested Grandpa. 'After all, Santa has to give lots of boys and girls presents.'

'Did you wish for anything Max?' asked Sophie.

'Yea, I wished for a big box of science experiments with one that can make little brothers disappear!' Everyone laughed and Harry hoped he was joking.

'What about you Soph, did you wish for anything special?' asked Grandpa.

'Yes, but it won't come true. I wished for a puppy.'

'Dad says no to puppies, you should have

wished for something else,' said Max.

Annoyingly, Sophie knew he was right, but she didn't want to hear it. She concentrated on enjoying her dinner – Gran's meals were always the best.

Everyone had cleared their mac and cheese plates and started tucking into apple crumble when the front door opened.

'Hello!' called Mum.

'Hi,' they all chorused through mouthfuls of pudding.

'That was a long journey today,' said Dad. Sophie saw him smile at Mum and she was sure he had winked too. Secrets, she thought. 'Dinner looks good, is there any left for a hungry Mum and Dad?'

'Of course.' Sophie watched as Gran came back with two plates of macaroni cheese.

'Oh, delicious, thank you! Just what I need. This'll give me energy to get three children in bed and milk out for Santa coming,' said Mum.

Sophie helped Gran clear the table. She liked helping Gran. Going into the lounge, she found Harry on the floor with his Lego and Max chatting to Grandpa. Mum and Dad were talking to one another. Sophie stepped over the boys and looked through the curtains at the snowman and the twinkling stars. It was so pretty. A perfect Christmas Eve.

'I think it's time for bed,' said Dad. 'Santa's coming, come on, let's get organised – cookies, milk, space for presents?'

'I'm on it, Dad,' said Harry, stuffing the Lego in the box as he raced Max to the kitchen to find milk and cookies.

Sophie laughed at Harry's silly walk as he came back from the kitchen carrying a plate of cookies. He carefully put them on the little table next to the tree and Max placed the milk and a carrot beside them.

'For you Santa, with love,' said Harry, bowing as he left the table. 'Race you!' he shouted as he sped off up the stairs. Max and Sophie followed, Max trying to grab his ankles. 'I'm too fast for you, slowcoaches!' Harry said as he reached the top stair.

'Night, night Sophie,' Max and Harry shouted.

'Night Max, night Harry, sleep tight and don't let the bed bugs bite,' she said as she headed into her room. As she got ready for bed, she heard Gran's footsteps on the stairs.

'Here's a Christmas stocking for Santa to leave some little presents in,' said Gran as she peeped round her door.

'Thanks Gran, see you for breakfast in the morning.'

'We think we'll come over early tomorrow and let Aunty Claire see you opening your presents.'

Sophie smiled. 'Love you Gran,' she said as she cuddled down into her warm bed, being careful not to kick the stocking off.

She wondered what Christmas morning might bring for her and her brothers. Poor Harry – would he dream about disappearing brothers? No doubt Max would be dreaming about science experiments. She closed her eyes and smiled.

Sophie was soon dreaming of big wrapped presents with matching bows under the Christmas tree.

Chapter 2
Christmas Morning

Sophie woke early to the sound of her brothers' voices.

'Max, are you sleeping?' she heard Harry whisper loudly. Before Max could answer, Harry shouted, 'Look! Our stockings are full, Santa's been!'

There was a thump on the floor as both boys jumped out of bed. Sophie cuddled down under her duvet and shut her eyes.

'Sophie, are you awake?' whispered Harry. She pretended to be asleep, opening only one eye before smiling at her brothers who couldn't wait and jumped on her bed with their stockings.

Everyone began taking little parcels out of their stockings and ripping them open. 'Wow, look at this!' said Harry over and over again. No-one was listening.

Paper was everywhere, and piles of little

presents were all over Sophie's bed. Harry was diving under the duvet, struggling to find his presents underneath all the wrapping paper.

'Ouch Harry – you're kicking me,' said Sophie.

'Sorry,' he mumbled.

At last, there was his pile – small boxes of Lego, chocolate, a read-it-yourself book, a puzzle and a satsuma! There was always a satsuma at the bottom of your stocking. Harry liked the chocolate better – it tasted good and Christmas day and Easter were the only days of the year he was allowed to eat chocolate at breakfast.

Stockings emptied, Sophie ran after her brothers as they headed through to Mum and Dad's room.

'Look what we have in our stockings! Can we go downstairs now, pleeasse?' asked Harry

Dad smiled. 'Haven't you been lucky? Okay, I'll go downstairs first, put the lights on and check Santa really has left some parcels. Just give me a minute.'

Sophie stood excitedly with her brothers at the top of the stairs waiting for Dad to tell them to come down. Harry couldn't keep still and spun round and round while Max looked intently at the foot of the stairs, waiting for Dad to shout. He was taking a long time.

The doorbell rang and Gran, Grandpa and Aunty Claire appeared. They were very early thought Sophie.

'Okay, I can see parcels,' said Dad and she was sure he winked at Grandpa. Secrets again. Sophie joined in as Max and Harry went racing down the stairs. They rushed past Gran and Grandpa and started running round all the piles of parcels, looking for their names. Harry, who was always the fastest, found his first. Paper was flying as though it had wings.

'Look Grandpa – a gigantic box of Lego! We

can build a whole village with this box!'

'And I've got my science experiments!' cried Max. Harry looked over nervously and Grandpa laughed.

'Don't worry, he doesn't have anything to make little brothers disappear!'

'What has Santa brought for you Sophie?' Mum asked.

'New pyjamas with a dog on the front and this box – it's very big but it isn't very heavy.' Sophie shook it, but it didn't seem to have anything inside. Strange, she thought as she began to rip the paper off. What could it be?

There was nothing inside the box, just a piece of paper lying at the bottom. She picked it up, opened it and began to read aloud...

> Dear Sophie,
>
> My elves have been watching you very carefully and you seem to be a very caring girl, so I have left you a very special present in the back garden.
>
> You will have to care for it.
>
> Don't let me down.
>
> Love from Santa x

Puzzled, Sophie ran to the back door and everyone followed. What kind of present would be left in the garden? Dad opened the door and there, where the snowman had been yesterday, Sophie saw a little wooden shed. She heard some sounds coming from it and ran over and opened the door. A ball of golden fluff jumped out and started barking very excitedly.

'It's a puppy!' shouted Sophie as she fell

backwards, trying to catch the beautiful puppy who was now running round the garden. Sophie ran after it shouting, 'It's a puppy, a beautiful puppy!'

'A dog?' said Max, looking astonished. 'Did Santa not know you didn't want a dog, Dad? Wow!' Max couldn't quite believe that shooting stars actually did make wishes come true. His Dad seemed to like dogs now.

AMAZING!

Sophie saw Gran and Grandpa smiling as she tried to catch her new puppy. But what did Dad think? She looked nervously over to see. Dad seemed to be smiling too. Sophie felt relieved.

After a few minutes, the puppy found the back door and ran into the house and everyone ran after him.

He disappeared underneath the piles of wrapping paper, only a squeaky little bark could be heard and then a head appeared. And off he dived again as Sophie and Grandpa gathered up all the paper, laughing as they tried to find him.

'Oh dear,' said Dad, looking a little worried. 'Let's think of a name so we can call him.'

'Sam, I like Sam,' said Sophie.

'What about Bonzo?' said Harry laughing.

'Sam's a good name – try it out and see if he likes it,' Grandpa suggested.

'Sam, come here,' called Sophie, and amazingly Sam ran straight to her.

Grandpa smiled. 'That's settled then, Sam it is.'

Sophie laughed as Sam ran from Harry to Max to her, tugging at paper and helping to pull at the parcels.

'Here Sam, help me,' shouted Harry.

'No Sam, help me,' shouted Max.

And of course, Sam wasn't really listening to anyone, he was just running and jumping. His tail was wagging so hard Sophie thought he might take off. She couldn't believe this cute little puppy was hers!

'You are a lucky girl Sophie, he is a beautiful puppy,' said Aunty Claire, sitting on the floor with Sophie and Sam. Sam bounced up and clambered onto Aunty Claire's legs. 'Oh, you're a lovely boy,' she said, tickling his back as Sam licked her other hand.

'I know! I didn't think Dad liked dogs, but he must do,' said Sophie, rubbing Sam's tummy as he lay with his legs in the air.

'Oh, your dad probably just thinks it's a lot of work to have a dog, but you're a good girl Sophie, you'll be fine with him. Let's take him out to the garden,' said Aunty Claire, standing up and sliding Sam carefully off her legs.

Sophie stood up too and Sam ran off to see Harry.

'Don't pick him up, he's going to the garden,' said Sophie.

'Don't be mean Sophie, he just wants a wee play,' said Harry, picking Sam up. 'Aw, Sam,' he said, putting the puppy straight back onto the floor. 'I'm all wet, yuck!'

'Told ya!' said Sophie.

'Go and get changed Harry and bring down the wet clothes,' said Mum.

Sophie opened the back door and Sam ran

out, running round the whole garden, sniffing at all the bushes and wagging his tail. Every so often, he seemed to sit down as though he was doing a pee.

'I think Sam's a girl – he keeps sitting down to do a pee,' said Max.

Aunty Claire laughed. 'No, no, he will cock his leg when he is a bit older, it's just like you used to sit on a potty. Then you learned to stand like a big boy.'

'Oh, okay,' said Max. 'It's getting chilly, I think we should head back in – if we can catch Sam,' laughed Aunty Claire.

Max ran towards the house. 'Come on Sam, we're boys,' he shouted, and to Sophie's surprise, Sam ran in after him.

Sophie sat on the floor beside Sam, picking him up and sitting him on her legs. As she tickled his ears, he settled down and lay stretched out, falling fast asleep.

'Aw, look at Sam,' said Harry, about to

poke him.

'Don't you dare, leave him alone,' said Sophie. 'He's tired.'

'Ooh, bossy Sophie,' said Harry, walking away and making a face.

'Just ignore him Soph,' said Max, sitting down beside her. Sophie sighed –she wanted Harry and Max to like her puppy too.

Chapter 3
Christmas Dinner

'Sophie, maybe we can try putting Sam in his cage if he's happy to go in there,' said Mum. 'Dinner in twenty minutes.'

Sophie checked the clock. She found her bag of puppy treats and put two inside the cage and then, two minutes before dinner, she brought Sam in and showed him the treats. He thought for a minute and then jumped into the cage.

'Clever boy, Sam!' said Sophie as she closed the door.

Sam stuck his nose through the crate and two big eyes looked back at Sophie. She put two more treats in his cage which Sam munched without any hesitation before flopping down. Everyone settled down at the table. Sophie sat between Grandpa and Aunty Claire. The table looked beautiful with Christmas flowers in the middle and crackers at everyone's place.

'Pull mine,' said Harry, stretching across the table to Max. Everyone looked at Sam, but he didn't seem to mind the cracker bang so everyone else pulled theirs too. Hats went on.

'What do you call a snowman's dog?' said Grandpa.

'Don't know,' shouted Max and Harry together.

'A slush puppy,' said Grandpa.

'Here's mine. Who delivers your dog's Christmas presents?' said Max

'Don't know,' said Gran.

'Santa paws,' laughed Max

'Soup,' said Dad as he put the hot bowls down and the jokes continued. Sam lay sleeping, his eyes opening at times and then closing again. All the chatter at the table didn't seem to disturb him. He seemed quite content in his cage. Sophie thought he was tired after all his running about.

Next, Dad carried turkey to his place at

the table while Mum brought bowls of vegetables and roast potatoes and Gran fetched the pigs in blankets, cranberry sauce and stuffing. The table was looking very full. The smell was amazing noses twitched as Dad carved the turkey and Grandpa gave out the plates. Soon everyone was adding food from the steaming bowls on the table and tucking into a delicious dinner.

'Oh, that was amazing! My tummy is stuffed,' said Aunty Claire, patting her tummy. 'Not sure I have space for pudding just now.'

Sam was now wide awake and whimpering as he stuck his nose through his crate.

'What if we have a wee break and a party game now, and pudding later?' suggested Mum and everyone agreed.

'Sophie, I cut a small slice of turkey for Sam and cut it up small with some pieces of carrot – that will be Christmas dinner for him,' said Dad.

'Thanks Dad,' said Sophie, getting Sam's

dish. 'You're a lucky boy Sam,' she said as she opened his cage and prepared his dinner. 'Here you go, yum yum,' she said as she put his dish down. Sam didn't need to be told twice, his nose was straight into the bowl. The turkey and carrots mix was a big success.

'Let's have the memory game, no-one needs to run about for this one,' said Dad, carrying a tray through and putting it on the coffee table. Sophie loved this game – she had a good memory, but so did Max.

'Harry, you play with me, you can help me remember and I will help you with the writing,' said Grandpa.

All eyes were focused on the tray as everyone concentrated. Two minutes later, Dad took it away and everyone started writing. It was always twenty things on the tray. Sophie was feeling pleased with herself – she had remembered seventeen.

'Stop, swap papers,' said Dad as he put the tray in the middle of the floor. That was a big mistake! Sam was back and had spotted the tray and was right in the middle of it.

'Stop Sam,' said Sophie, trying to lift him out from all the scattered objects. But Sam seemed really pleased with himself, his tail wagging furiously as he ran away with the duster.

'Oh no! I forgot we had a puppy,' said Dad as he lifted the tray onto the sideboard and gathered up all the objects.

'Good job, Sam, your name should be Demolition Dan!' said Max, laughing and catching him. Max sat down on the floor and played tug of war with the duster Sam had stolen from the tray.

Sophie watched Harry eyeing up Aunty Claire's prize – she had remembered eighteen objects and been declared the winner. 'Aunty Claire, do you like those sweets?' he asked.

'I do, but I will share them after pudding.

We all had good scores,' winked Aunty Claire. Harry gave her a high five.

'Oh Sophie, Sam's ripped Mum's duster,' said Max. 'Naughty Sam.'

'Silly Max,' said Dad as he came back into the lounge. Harry laughed – it was usually him being silly.

'Christmas karaoke anyone?' said Dad.

'Jingle bells, jingle bells, jingle all the way,' Max and Sophie sang together, pretending they had mics.

'Okay, give me a minute to set it up. Who's first?' said Dad

'Me!' shouted Grandpa. The whole family loved singing. 'Do you think Sam can sing?' said Grandpa, giving him a wee tickle behind his ears.

Sophie watched Sam who was sitting on the floor chewing his rope.

Grandpa stood up. 'He's done it again,' he laughed, looking at his shoes. His laces were undone; it was the second time today that Sam had pulled them out. Grandpa bent down and tied them again.

Grandpa began to sing his favourite song, 'White Christmas', but Sam was not impressed – he lay down with his head on the floor and put his front paws over his ears!

'Look at Sam!' said Harry, laughing.

Grandpa laughed too. 'Well I guess he wants me to stop. Time for pudding I think.'

With full tummies after pudding, no-one had the energy for any more games.

'TV for a wee while,' said Dad, picking up the remote. Everyone settled down including Sam who just wandered from person to person looking for tickles and cuddles as they all watched Gran's favourite programme, the 'Strictly Christmas Special'.

'I've had such a lovely day, but I think I need to go home to my bed now,' said Grandpa, stretching his legs out. 'A new puppy has exhausted us all,' he said, smiling at Sophie. 'I'll get our coats.'

'I'll do it,' said Harry, running up the stairs.

'Bye,' they all shouted as Gran, Grandpa and Aunty Claire left.

Mum and Dad sat in the lounge and Max and Harry sat on the floor with Harry's new Lego set while Sam pushed the bits about with his paws.

'Careful Sam,' said Harry, taking the bits back. Sam paid no attention and pushed other pieces with his nose.

Sophie picked Sam up, holding him a little off her dress just in case, and headed out to the garden. When they came back, she put a toilet mat in his cage, he would need the toilet during the night, and some treats to persuade him to go In. He seemed happy going into his cage and she sat on the floor beside him until he fell fast asleep. She would leave her bedroom door open in case he was whining during the night. He might be missing his mum and his brothers and sisters.

Chapter 4
Hogmanay

Sophie tickled Sam as they lay on the floor together. She could hardly believe Sam had been her puppy for a whole week. Her puppy book was really useful with the training tips and explaining how to look after a puppy but it didn't tell you about untying shoelaces, or that table legs might have tiny teeth marks in them or about pulling towels off hooks. He was a busy puppy – a very busy puppy who only stopped when he was sleeping.

Today was a special day – the very last day of the year, the 31st of December. Sophie liked Hogmanay. Mum and Dad always had a fun party and the neighbours came to visit and stayed for the midnight bells. Sophie hoped Sam would be well-behaved – so far, he seemed to like people.

The party preparations had started. Mum and Gran were chatting as they polished and dusted before cleaning the kitchen and the lounge – apparently, according to Mum and Gran, it was very important to have a clean house to bring in the New Year. She wondered if Victoria and her mum were busy cleaning next door too.

Dad was making a big steak pie, which was to be the midnight meal, and Grandpa was putting out glasses and drinks on the sideboard in the lounge – one side for grown-up drinks and the other side for kids' drinks. Harry was helping Grandpa, probably in the hope he would be allowed some of his favourite Irn-Bru.

Sophie was helping Max put books and games away. Sam was running around as fast as he could, carrying an assortment of toys and hoping someone would stop and play with him. Grandpa laughed but Dad was not happy.

'Sam, you are being a very silly dog, go to your bed,' he said.

Sam looked a bit sad and thought about running back to Sophie, but Dad said loudly, 'Bed Sam, now.'

Sophie put Sam in his bed but she saw that he was keeping an eye on Dad in case he changed his mind. 'We'll play soon,' she whispered to him.

'I think we'll put Sam's bed in your room, just for tonight,' Dad said to Sophie.

'Sam, Sam, you're sleeping in my room tonight!' said Sophie, hugging him.

Sam didn't understand a word she was saying – he thought it was a new game and jumped out of his bed, ready to play. Sam was back to running around and had brought Gran's shoe into the lounge. Oh no, thought Sophie.

'Sam, come and help me put away these books,' she said, hoping no-one would notice as she lifted Sam up and ran up the stairs, delighted to have him to herself.

Once in her room, Sam put his paws up

onto her duvet which was hanging over the edge of the bed. He wasn't big enough yet to be able to jump up by himself. Sophie lifted him onto the bed and he flopped down. Sophie laughed. 'Are you tired, Sam? You have a wee rest. You are sleeping in here tonight.' She hoped there wouldn't be fireworks in case Sam was frightened. It was funny – she had liked them last year but this year she didn't want her little puppy to be scared. He didn't need much persuasion and in a few minutes he was curled up and fast asleep. As Sophie looked through her wardrobe for a dress to wear to the party, she heard some funny dog talk: 'Hmm, hmm, hmmm.' Sam was talking in his sleep! Sophie wondered if he was having a nice dream.

Before she headed downstairs, Sophie lifted Sam into his own bed on the floor. He seemed to be exhausted from all his running about and stayed curled up and fast asleep.

At last, all the jobs were finished and

everyone was laughing and chatting in the lounge.

'Takeaway tea?' suggested Mum.

'Pizza,' said Harry. Everyone agreed.

Dad called for two large pizzas, some chips and ice-cream. It was going to be a feast.

Sophie crept back upstairs. Peeking round the door, she saw that Sam was still in his bed, fast asleep. As she tiptoed into her room, his eyes flashed open and he jumped up. 'Hello Sam,' said Sophie. As she gave him a big cuddle, she heard Mum calling: 'Tea's here!'

Sophie pulled open her bedroom door and Sam shot out and plodded carefully down the stairs. Harry's lessons had paid off and Sam was improving on the stairs, though he was still faster at going up than coming down.

Sophie took him out to the garden for a pee after his big sleep and then popped him into his cage with a few treats while they had tea.

'Yum,' said Max, as they all sat down, 'my

favourite.'

'Mine too,' said Harry, taking a big pile of chips from the centre of the table.

'Want to hear a good joke?' he asked through a mouthful of chips. 'Knock, knock.'

'Who's there?' said Max.

'Tye,' said Harry.

'Tye who?'

'Tyrannosaurus wrecks everything that gets in his way!' laughed Harry.

'Good joke Harry, but let's focus on our food – we still have to choose our party outfits,' said Mum.

The family quickly finished off the pizza feast. 'Alright everyone, who's going to help me tidy up?' Mum asked as she started to clear the table.

'Aw, boring,' said Harry. 'Sam and I are going to play tug of war with his rope.'

Harry slid along the floor to Sam's toy box

and Sam ran after him, being pulled along the carpet with all four paws out, his teeth sunk into Harry's joggers.

'I don't know who's more silly,' laughed Dad.

There was plenty of time for choosing outfits and a wee nap before the guests arrived. The Hogmanay party didn't start until ten o'clock at night.

Sophie had decided to wear the new blue dress which Gran and Grandpa had bought her for Christmas. She had a wee blue ribbon she would tie onto Sam's collar so that he had a special outfit too – that's if he stood still long enough for her to tie it on. Grandpa would be wearing his tartan trews as he always did at New Year and Gran would have on her green velvet dress – they loved to wear special outfits.

Everyone was almost ready for their guests. Mum was putting fresh hand towels in the bathroom and Gran was lighting candles which smelled of Christmas trees; Grandpa was checking the drinks table and Dad was keeping an eye on the oven. Sam was running round everyone, delivering toys to their feet and trying to climb up onto the couch, but his little legs were just not long enough yet.

Victoria from next door was coming with her mum Emily, and their neighbours John and Heather from number six would be bringing their son Colin who was one of Harry's friends.

Sophie watched as Sam barked and wagged his tail at each guest who came in. Victoria brought him some treats and Sam followed her around.

'You're so funny, Sam, I wish I had a puppy like you,' said Victoria, giving him a big cuddle. The party was going well – all the grown-ups were chatting and laughing, and the children were playing with Sam who was loving all the attention.

He chased toys through legs, ran round behind the furniture to find hidden toys and enjoyed some play fighting with Harry. Sophie was so glad he was friendly. Her puppy book said that it was very important to mix with new people and tonight was a perfect occasion.

As Dad was taking the steak pie out of the oven and putting food out, Sophie noticed that Sam had started to behave a bit strangely. He kept climbing up to the top of the stairs and barking. He then plodded back down and sat at Sophie's side. Sophie was a bit surprised. Maybe he didn't like the smell of the food, she thought.

The third time he did it, Dad said, 'Sophie, if Sam barks again, he has to go to bed.'

'That's not like him Sophie, is he okay?' said Grandpa.

A minute later, Sam was back at the top of the stairs and barking again. She didn't understand what he was doing.

Getting up, Sophie said, 'Sam, what's wrong with you? Why are you barking? Dad is getting annoyed.' As Sophie reached the top of the stairs, she noticed that Max and Harry's bedroom door was open and the light was on. As she approached the door, she could see Colin sitting on the bedroom floor. He was crying.

'Colin, what's wrong? Why are you crying?' asked Sophie.

'I came up to play with some Lego and I've mixed it all up and I don't know how to sort it. Mum and Dad and Harry will be cross with me,' sobbed Colin.

'No they won't, Colin. Harry mixes his Lego up all the time, he's really good at sorting it. Don't worry, he won't mind. We'll tell him together, come on. Let's go back downstairs and join the others. Don't cry, it really doesn't matter.'

'Really?' asked Colin, still sniffing. Sam gave him a wee nudge with his nose and popped his two front paws on Colin's legs. 'Thank you, Sam, you're nice,' he said as he cuddled him. He stood up and followed Sam and Sophie back down the stairs.

'Good boy Sam, you were a very clever puppy, letting me know about Colin,' Sophie whispered, giving Sam a great big cuddle as she sat back down in the lounge.

'Is everything alright?' asked Dad. 'Has Sam stopped barking?'

'Everything's fine Dad.'

Sophie and Colin told Harry about the Lego. 'That's okay, I mix it up for fun sometimes. If you want, you can come and play tomorrow and we can sort it,' said Harry.

Sophie smiled. Although Harry was a bit silly at times, he wasn't unkind and Sophie knew he wouldn't fuss about the Lego. Colin sat down beside Harry and joined in the charades guessing game. There were two teams and Grandpa was trying to describe a TV programme to his team which, looking at what he was doing with his arms and legs, was all about football.

'Sportscene!' shouted Harry, jumping up. 'My turn now.'

'Well done, but it's the other team now, Harry,' said Grandpa. 'You'll be next.'

Sophie noticed that Sam sat beside Colin until he tickled his ears and then moved on. He was such a kind puppy, she thought. Sam loved the party and all the people.

'Drinks everyone,' said Dad, 'it's almost time for the bells.'

He switched on the television for the big countdown. Dad had said no to fireworks this year in case they scared Sam, so they were going to watch them on the TV instead.

The countdown started. 'Ten... nine... eight... seven... six... five... four... three... two... HAPPY NEW YEAR!' shouted everyone all at the same time. Sam ran round and round Sophie's legs, barking as everyone hugged and wished each other 'Happy New Year'.

Mum sent John out through the back door with a bottle of whisky in one hand and a cake in the other. She was letting the old year out and John, who had the darkest hair, had to go round to the front and be the first foot. Sophie would never be allowed to be the first foot as she had fair hair and Grandpa said dark-haired people would bring good luck.

When John was safely back in the house, Dad put on some Scottish music and the children all had to do a Highland Fling. Grandpa was going to choose the best. Sophie thought that Victoria who went to dancing lessons was really the best, but Grandpa said everyone was excellent and they all got gold chocolate medals.

Then it was the adults' turn to dance. Sophie laughed as she watched – Grandpa was

was good he had rhythm, but Dad was terrible, he looked like a windmill.

When the neighbours left, Sophie headed for bed, taking Sam up with her. She changed into her pyjamas, brushed her teeth and tucked Sam up in his bed. As she sat on the floor beside him, she thought about tonight. Sam was good at learning and maybe she was imagining it, but she was sure he had noticed that Colin was upset. She was amazed such a little puppy could be so kind and felt very proud of Sam.

He was soon fast asleep in his bed on her floor and she climbed into bed too. She closed her eyes and thought about the puppy classes where she would learn even more new things with Sam.

Chapter 5
Sam Settles In

Now that the new year had begun, it would only be a few more days until Sophie went back to school. Life was both fantastic and chaotic now that Sam was here.

She smiled as she heard Sam whining as he climbed the stairs. He was looking for someone to play with. She hid underneath her duvet, peeking out just at the edge to see a nose and then a furry body followed by a wagging tail appearing round her door. She waited and, sure enough, two paws followed by a nose and two beady eyes slid under the duvet – Sam was not to be fooled. Sophie lifted him up beside her. 'Oh Sam,' she laughed as she sat up. 'Did you know I was here? Clever puppy,' she said as she tickled his tummy.

'Sophie, Sam needs to go into the garden and you need to get up,' shouted Dad.

'I'm up, just coming down,' said Sophie as

she pulled on her onesie and slippers – a wet bed wasn't the best idea.

She walked carefully down the stairs with Sam who was taking them two at a time 0– he was definitely getting faster. He would be beating Harry soon. She smiled at him, thinking how lucky she was to be given such an amazing present. She knew it meant hard work too – she wanted him to be the best puppy ever.

Dad smiled as she passed by and Sophie knew he was pleased that she was looking after Sam so well. She had heard him say to Mum last night, 'Sophie is really trying to learn with Sam, I think they will be fine together.'

As she pulled the back door open, she could feel the icy blast from the cold January air. The bushes glistened in the morning frost. Soon they would go to the vet's for Sam's puppy jabs and then he could go out for walks.

She shivered as Sam ran around, smiling

as she remembered Harry showing Sam how to lift his leg when he was doing a little pee. She laughed as he wobbled and toppled then got up and ran on. He was learning quickly.

As she watched him, she wondered what Grandpa would say this afternoon. He was coming round to chat with her about how he could help with Sam when she went back to school next week. Sophie felt a bit worried about leaving Sam. It had been the Christmas holidays and he was used to her being here all the time; she wondered if he would get lonely when she went back to school. He had only lived with her for ten days and already she loved him so much. Harry and Max loved him too.

Sophie laughed – Sam was now ready to play, jumping in front of her and hoping she would chase him. Sophie ran and Sam ran too; she threw his rope toy and he chased after it, running at the speed of light.

She heard the back door open and turned to see Harry dressed in a warm jacket and carrying a soft sponge ball. 'Football, Sam?' he said as he kicked the ball along the grass. Sophie wasn't sure Sam understood football, but he loved chasing Harry and the ball.

'I'm going in to get dressed but play fair Harry, he needs a shot of the ball please?' said Sophie, heading for the back door. Harry grinned; Sophie was sure Sam wouldn't get fair play, but he would get some exercise. Harry was very serious when it came to football. And Harry's sponge ball might not survive if Sam got his little teeth into it.

As Sophie came back downstairs, she saw Harry coming back in with Sam. 'It's chilly, Sam told me he was cold,' he said.

Poor Sam, she thought as he flumped down in his bed. Soon she heard puppy snores from his cage – he was exhausted from his football with Harry. But she knew it probably wouldn't take too long before his energy levels were topped back up. Sam was a bit like the new baby across the road – sleeping for a while then bright as button, running round everyone's legs with his toys.

Just as she finished setting the table for lunch, the doorbell rang. That would be Grandpa – his timing always seemed to be just perfect, lunch was almost ready. Sam heard the bell and was up like a shot and off to the door to say hello. He was quicker than Harry and Max. 'Woah Sam,' said Harry as he stumbled, trying not to stand on Sam as he ran through his legs.

'Well hello, this is a lovely welcome,' said Gran, bending down to pat Sam. 'Three children and an excited puppy, I feel very special.'

Sophie took Gran's and Grandpa's jackets and ran upstairs to put them on her bed. Just as she was putting them down, Sam appeared beside the jackets.

'Sam!' she said, astonished that he had

managed to jump up there. He hadn't done that before. 'Clever boy! Now, can you get back down?' she said, gently pushing him towards the floor. He gave her a cute look and did as he was told, running back down the stairs, game over.

'Guess what Sam's just done!' said Sophie as she popped him into his cage. 'He can jump onto my bed.'

'Can I see?' said Harry.

'Later,' said Dad as they all sat round the table.

'He's a good boy Sophie, lying in his bed while we eat lunch,' said Grandpa. 'You don't want a dog that looks for food while everyone is eating, that's not good behaviour. Very wise to start when he is a puppy, then he will always do it.'

'It was Dad's idea,' said Sophie. 'I didn't realise it was important.'

'I expect we will need a few family rules so that Sam doesn't get mixed messages and become confused about what he is allowed to do. The puppy classes will help with that I expect,' said Grandpa.

'I wonder if there are behaviour classes for children,' laughed Dad, looking at Harry.

'Not funny, Dad,' shouted Harry. 'I'm as good as gold, most of the time.'

'Children aren't supposed to be good all the time – your dad wasn't,' said Gran, winking at Harry. 'But he's quite well behaved now.' Everyone laughed.

Sophie watched Dad smile at Gran, who was smiling straight back at him. Gran saw everyone's good bits – she always said it was a gran's job to love her grandchildren even when they were naughty. Sophie looked at Gran and Grandpa and felt lucky.

Once the table had been cleared, she sat with Grandpa to go through all the things he would need to do to help with Sam.

'Okay love, what's first?' he asked.

'Well, you've to use these bags to pick up his poo,' said Sophie nervously.

Grandpa laughed. 'Don't worry, I've changed a lot of nappies, I can do poo bags.' Sophie laughed too.

'He gets treats to help him learn,' said Sophie. 'Sam!' she shouted and Sam ran over. 'Look, I'm teaching him to sit. Sit Sam,' she said and moved her hand with the treat down and Sam sat. 'Good boy. He doesn't always do it but he's getting better and he follows the treats. I learned it on YouTube. There are some good training videos.'

'Okay, show me on the computer,' said Grandpa.

Sophie fetched the laptop and Grandpa settled down to watch the videos. Sophie left him to it and went back into the lounge. She smiled to see her brothers playing with the puppy.

'Here Sam,' said Max, sitting on the floor as

he threw Sam's teddy over to Harry who was sitting opposite him. Sam ran over and of course Harry threw the teddy back. Sophie was just about to rescue Sam when Harry threw the teddy a bit lower and Sam managed to catch it. He ran off and sat beside Dad.

'Good boy, Sam,' said Dad and Sam snuggled down on top of his feet.

'Good videos, Soph,' said Grandpa as he came into the lounge. 'I think you're doing really well. I'll come round at lunchtime each day and spend some time with Sam.'

Sophie was feeling nervous – it was only a few more days until she went back to school. Grandpa was sure Sam would be just fine in his cage with a treat and some toys and a bowl of water until he came over to let him into the garden and play with him. Sophie hoped so – she knew she was lucky to have Grandpa to help.

Realising Sam wasn't in the lounge

anymore, Sophie went looking for him. She found him snuggling into Max and enjoying a story about spaceships. It looked like he knew that Max liked books – he often took a ball to Harry but he seemed much calmer around Max. She wondered if a little puppy could sense that people were different. She did notice that he often sat at Dad's feet until Dad patted him and said, 'Good boy, Sam.' Then he would run off. Was he training Dad?

She smiled as Sam stretched out his legs, looking at Max to tickle his tummy, which he did as he continued to read. 'Clever me, Sam, I can tickle and read at the same time,' laughed Max.

Sophie went upstairs to get her puppy training book. As she reached the top step, she heard two barks and wondered what was wrong. She skipped back down the stairs and found Sam at the back door. She opened it and he ran out and had a pee.

'Grandpa, did you hear him bark twice?'

asked Sophie.

'Yes love, I did. Does he always do that?'

'I don't think so,' said Sophie.

'Very smart for his age,' said Grandpa, watching Sam running around some bushes. 'He'll be an interesting one to watch grow up, Sophie.'

'I think so too Grandpa. He seems to like living at 2 Ashgrove Terrace,' said Sophie.

Chapter 6
At The Vet's

Sophie skipped down the stairs two at a time, headed into the kitchen and opened Sam's cage. He lifted his head and jumped straight out, wagging his tail and running round her in great big circles.

'Hello Sam! You're the best puppy ever,' she said as she cuddled him. 'Today, we'll visit the vet for your puppy injections. It's a big day – after that, we're going to the park for the first time!' She could hardly wait, she felt as excited as Sam.

As she opened the back door and Sam ran out, she felt a cold blast of frosty air wrap around her like an ice blanket. The grass sparkled like soft glitter on a Christmas card – early February was just as cold as December.

Morning pee achieved, Sam ran about sniffing the snowdrops which were beginning to pop their white heads through; he was getting better at going outside for the toilet – there were hardly any accidents in the house now. After today, she would be able to take Sam for a walk before school and not just stand in the cold in her pyjamas.

'Sophie,' shouted Mum, 'Grandpa is on the phone for you.'

Sophie took the phone from Mum. 'Hi Grandpa.' Sophie listened. 'Yes, I'll hurry home from school and be waiting for you. Bye Grandpa, thank you.' How was she going to concentrate at school today? She was far too excited. And it was spelling test day; she crossed her fingers.

Sophie knew that Grandpa was a really good help and she felt very lucky to have such a kind grandpa. So far, the Monday to Friday routine of Grandpa visiting Sam was working well – Sam seemed happy and Grandpa was enjoying Sam's fun. They would often read her puppy book together and soon they would all be going to puppy classes. Sophie often wondered when she watched Grandpa with Sam why Dad was not so keen on dogs when his own dad liked them so much. Sam would change Dad's mind she thought.

Sophie called Sam in as she sorted his breakfast out; he circled her legs, making sure she knew he was hungry.

'Good boy, Sam,' she said, as she put his bowl on the floor before heading back to her room to put on her school clothes and check her school bag. Mrs Johnstone was her class teacher and she was her favourite teacher so far, she was excited that she could tell her about Sam going out to the park today.

'Bye Sam, big day later, love you,' she said as she kissed him goodbye and set off for school with Max, Harry and Victoria.

It felt like the longest day ever. At the three o'clock bell, Sophie was first out of class and ran all the way home. She remembered Mr Smith, the vet, visiting a school assembly one day last year to talk about looking after your pet. She wished she'd had a puppy that day.

'Hi Grandpa,' said Sophie as she rushed through the front door. 'I thought I'd let Sam out for a pee before we go,' she shouted as she put her school bag down.

'Good idea,' said Grandpa. 'Then I think we'll head up to the vet.'

Sophie watched Sam running and jumping in the garden and dropping a ball he had found under a bush at her feet. She threw it across the garden and off Sam ran at full speed. He was getting good at this game. She put the ball into her pocket and picked up Sam's lead. 'Game over, Sam,' she said as he followed her into the kitchen.

She climbed into the back of Grandpa's car with Sam and tickled his ears. 'Not long now, Sam,' she said.

Sophie felt a bit nervous as she carried Sam into the vet's. It was a first for them both.

'Hello Sophie,' said the lady behind the desk. 'I'm Lucy. When your dad called to make the appointment, he said you'd be bringing Sam. Maybe your grandpa could fill in these forms for me while you and Sam go in and see Mr Smith.'

Sophie saw the forms on a large wooden desk which was in front of rows of medicines, all lined up neatly on the shelves. Sophie wondered how anyone could remember the names of all those medicines, there were so many. She hoped Sam wouldn't need any.

She put Sam down and saw a sign on a white wooden door: 'MR SMITH'. Sophie pushed the door open and Sam ran in.

'Hello, are you Sophie and is this Sam?' said Mr Smith who was wearing a white coat a bit like a hospital doctor.

'Yes,' said Sophie. 'My grandpa is filling in

forms with Lucy.'

'Excellent, let me have a look at Sam and then we will give him his injection. Can you put him on the table please?' Sophie caught Sam, lifted him up and put him on the large silver table. Sam didn't look too sure and Sophie thought he might jump off but Mr Smith held him gently and Sam gave him a doggy kiss

'Nice friendly dog you have Sophie.'

Sophie felt really proud as Sam stood very still when Mr Smith checked his mouth and his ears and felt along his tummy and legs. He took his temperature by putting a small white machine at his ear.

'He seems healthy Sophie, he just needs his injections now. This is actually his second injection as he had his first before he left his mum. It will be another two weeks before he can go outside the garden or the house,' said Mr Smith as he prepared the injection.

'Two weeks?' said Sophie – she hadn't expected that news. She could feel tears spring to her eyes.

'It takes two weeks for the injection to work and you don't want him to get a nasty virus. He is such a lovely puppy.'

'Thank you, Mr Smith,' said Sophie, blinking back the tears and taking Sam back out to Grandpa.

'Well, is everything okay?' asked Grandpa.

'Yes, everything is fine, Grandpa. Mr Smith says Sam is healthy, but I need to keep him in for two more weeks and I don't want to.'

'Oh, two weeks will pass quickly and it's best to be safe,' said Grandpa.

'I know, but I don't want to wait two more weeks. I wanted to take him to the park today,' said Sophie. She picked Sam up to take him back to the car.

'Bye Sophie, bye Sam,' said Lucy from

behind her desk.

'Bye,' said Sophie and Sam gave a bark goodbye. Lucy laughed.

'You are a very good boy. I'm sorry we can't go to the park today,' said Sophie, giving Sam a cuddle and a wee treat.

'He will go to the park soon, Sophie. We'll put a date in the calendar and then we will all have something to look forward to,' said Grandpa.

'But I want to go today. I told Fatima and Emma I was going and they were coming to see Sam.'

'You can phone your friends and explain, but you can't take Sam to the park today, you'll just have to be patient.'

'I know it's the right thing to do. I just wish it was today,' sighed Sophie. She was beginning to realise that being responsible wasn't always fun. It was disappointing and she felt annoyed but at the same time she didn't want Sam to be unwell.

Emma and Fatima would be disappointed – she hoped they hadn't left for the park already. She knew that Harry and Max would be delighted – they loved playing with Sam in the garden. Sam could now sometimes catch the ball before Max or Harry, so the game was more of a challenge for them too. Sam was becoming bigger, faster and a little stronger. They were kind to Sam, even if they did tease him sometimes.

It was a real nuisance, but she would just have to wait two more weeks. It would be a long two weeks.

Chapter 7
Puppy Classes

'Last day!' said an excited Sophie, reaching over to the calendar and scoring off the final day of garden and house time.

Mum smiled. 'Tomorrow is the big day – Sam can go out for walks or to the park. You have been really patient, Sophie, well done. I hear you and Grandpa have got plans for tomorrow. It's good that it's a Saturday.'

'Yea, first puppy class in the morning and Grandpa says we can go for a walk in the afternoon.'

'That's a good idea and kind of Grandpa. The crocuses are out – can you ask Grandpa to take a photo of you and Sam beside them? I'll go shopping with Gran while you two are busy.'

Sophie laughed, she knew that meant Mum and Gran would be having lunch out. They liked their shopping and lunch days. Sophie liked the little treats that Gran often brought her back. She knew Harry would be at his football and Max would be standing at the side of the pitch, reading his book, waiting for Dad to take them to the bakery for hot pies and doughnuts.

Well, she would be having the best day with Grandpa. The puppy classes were just thirty minutes, but Grandpa said that was long enough for puppies. They were going to come home for some lunch before their walk. Exploring the village with Sam was going to be such fun – she had looked forward to this day for ages. She hoped some of her friends might be in the park too.

Next morning, she looked out of the window and was delighted to see no rain – it was a great day for a first walk with Sam. She pulled on her clothes and went downstairs to let Sam into the garden. As she was watching Sam, she heard the doorbell ring.

'Anyone for puppy classes?' called

Grandpa. Sam, recognising his voice, ran to meet him, giving one of his usual barks 'hello' before running off to sniff the plants again.

'Let's grab his lead and remember to take a bag of treats. The letter says we need them for training,' said Grandpa.

'Already on the worktop,' said Sophie who was feeling very excited. She was just having toast for breakfast – she had butterflies in her tummy and couldn't eat the rolls and sausages her brothers were tucking into. She was pleased Grandpa was going with her. She wasn't sure if she was nervous, excited or both. She grabbed her jacket from the hall and headed out to the car with Sam.

Grandpa's car stopped at the old church which had changed into a pet shop and puppy class centre. Sophie stepped out of the car with Sam, clipped on his lead and walked up the gravelly path, making a loud crunchy sound with every step. Sophie wondered how Sam would react when he saw other puppies. He was so friendly, he would probably just run round wagging his tail at everyone. She was glad he was on his lead because he was so fast, she wouldn't be able to catch him.

Grandpa walked beside her while Sam darted in and out of their legs, trying to run backwards and forwards. Sophie was struggling to keep him close as he pulled on the lead.

'Hello, can I have your names please?' asked the friendly man at the front door.

'This is Sam and I'm Sophie and this is my grandpa,' said Sophie, trying to hold Sam tightly as he was still trying to run off.

'Welcome! Sam's first class is in the garden at the back of the building, just through the double doors and straight out. Find a chair to sit on and keep Sam on the lead please. We'll start in a couple of minutes. Just one more puppy to come.' Sophie wondered how many puppies there would be.

As they walked into the garden, Sophie saw that four other owners and their puppies were already there. There was a black and white collie sitting nicely at the feet of a man with bushy hair and a beard, a white poodle sitting on the knee of a smiley lady, a chocolate labrador with a boy who looked about the same age as her, with maybe his mum, and a little white dog that she thought was a westie with a very beautiful lady.

Sophie sat in the chair next to the boy with the labrador. Grandpa put Sam in between their feet and they both tickled his ears to keep him calm. Just as they settled, the last dog appeared, a tiny little dog with a small nervous lady owner; the friendly man from the door came into the garden too.

The quietness suddenly exploded into noise as the westie and the tiny puppy started barking loudly at one another; all the other puppies joined in, making a deafening noise. No owner was having much success in getting their dog to be quiet. What a din thought Sophie.

'Welcome, I'm John and I'll be taking your classes,' he shouted above the barking. Slowly, the racket stopped as owners quietened their puppies.

'It's good to see everyone with their puppies. We'll start right away by introducing yourself. Please stand up when I ask and introduce yourself and your puppy. Keep the puppy on a short lead so that they can move about.' He was still having to speak quite loudly as both the westie and the little dog continued to bark at one another – or maybe they were just barking at everyone.

'Sophie, can you go first please?' asked John.

Sophie and Grandpa stood up. 'I'm Sophie

and this is Sam, he's a labradoodle, and this is my grandpa.'

The boy was next and Sophie learned that he was called Tom and his puppy was called Ben. Quickly, everyone else took their turn and introduced themselves. Sophie was too nervous to remember all the other names; she would ask Grandpa later.

'Today, we are going to learn the "sit" and "stand" commands and walking on a lead. To do this, stand up and face your puppy. Say the word sit and when your puppy sits, say good boy or girl and give them a treat.'

Sophie stood up and Sam began to run round her legs. The lead was winding tightly round her legs and she couldn't move. She almost fell over – what a start!

'Sam, sit,' said Sophie as she tried to unwind the lead. John came over and stood in front of Sam.

'Sit,' he said to Sam and Sam sat as John held out a treat. 'Now you do it Sophie.'

'Sit,' said Sophie, holding out a treat to Sam and amazingly he did sit. 'Well done Sam, you are a clever boy,' said Sophie. She tried three more times and Sam sat three times. 'You have a go too, Grandpa, he is really good.' Each time Sam sat, Sophie felt very proud of him.

'He learns quickly, Sophie, he's a clever dog,' said Grandpa.

Sophie noticed that at first, all the dogs were just running round their owners but after a few minutes and some treats, the other puppies were beginning to sit too. Except for the little dog, who was still barking. Sophie watched John trying to encourage the little dog to sit but he wasn't as obedient as the other puppies.

'Well done everyone, that was a great start. As we go through the classes, it is important to remember to be patient and kind with your puppy even when they are not being as obedient as you'd like. If they are not behaving, just distract them and then try again. Always give lots of praise for good behaviour, then your puppy will be a happy one.'

John spun round, looking at the group. 'Okay, next command. This time, ask your puppy to sit, give them a treat and then take one step to the side, say stand and your puppy should stand. Again, give them a treat as they stand. Off you go.'

Sophie stood and faced Sam. 'Sit,' she said clearly and was delighted when Sam sat. 'Clever boy,' she said, giving him a treat and a pat. Then she took a step to the side and said 'stand'. John was right – Sam did stand up. 'Oh, what a clever boy you are Sam,' she said as she gave him a cuddle and another treat. Sophie noticed that Tom was cuddling Ben too and when she looked round, most of the other owners were cuddling their puppies. Maybe the little dog wasn't so good, but John was helping. The lady still looked quite flustered.

'I'll try some more and then you try too, Grandpa,' said Sophie.

'Good idea,' said Grandpa, smiling.

Sam was beginning to get a little too excited and was standing when he should be sitting. Maybe it's time for Grandpa to have a go thought Sophie and handed him the lead. Sam was good for Grandpa and was standing and sitting at the right times again.

'Excellent everyone, amazing progress. The last thing to practise today is walking on the lead. I'll take Sam if that's okay Sophie and show everyone what to do. It is important to have control over your puppy when he's walking on the lead. They need to feel that you are in charge, it'll make them feel secure.'

John came over and took Sam's lead. 'Good boy Sam,' he said as he moved Sam over to his right side. 'It's important to choose a side, right or left, that your puppy will walk beside. Then use a phrase like "let's go" as the walk command. Give treats as they walk closely beside you.' Sam was the perfect puppy pupil – Sophie proudly watched her lovely bundle of fun doing everything John asked.

'Now, find a space behind your chair and try walking forward. We'll go in a clockwise direction.' Sam was being very good for John so Sophie knew he could do it.

'Thank you Sam,' said John as he gave Sam back to Sophie. 'Remember to put your puppy on your right or left as you like. Keep the lead short and use a command like "let's go". As your dog walks, remember to give him treats.'

The puppies were running backwards and forwards and their owners were running after them. It took quite a few minutes before darting puppies were walking in a circle. Well, except for the little dog, Angus, who had tangled his lead round a chair. As his owner unclipped the lead to untangle it, Angus took off! He ran excitedly up and down the garden with his owner and John running after him and calling – but Angus was not listening! Eventually, it was Tom who managed to catch him as he ran to see Ben. It was funny but Sophie was glad it wasn't Sam. Angus was going to be a lot of fun.

'That was a really good start for a first class. Keep practising for ten minutes every day but remember that puppies get tired quickly, so don't overdo it. See you all next week, when we will be teaching the puppies to respond to their name and the "wait" command.'

As they were leaving, Sam and Ben were sniffing one another. Sophie had enjoyed her first class and was pleased that Sam seemed to have found a friend.

'Phew, my brain is hurting! I think Sam and

I are both exhausted now, Grandpa,' said Sophie as they headed back to the car.

Grandpa laughed. 'Well, home for lunch and Sam can have a wee nap before we take him out for a walk. We can try it all again when we are out this afternoon.'

Sophie gave Grandpa a hug. 'Thanks Grandpa,' she said. She was looking forward to next week. Dad was right – it was good to learn things at puppy classes. The puppy book had good information, but the classes were helpful to see what to practise. She was pleased she had both.

'Cheese sandwich Grandpa?' said Sophie as they arrived home.

'Yes love, that sounds wonderful. I'll just put my feet up while you make lunch.'

Sophie noticed as she carried Grandpa's sandwiches through that Sam was in his bed. She went back to the kitchen and sat down on the floor beside his cage. He looked at her with one eye and then it closed too. He was fast asleep, his tummy rising and falling as he lay curled up in a ball. Sophie blew him a kiss and collected her own lunch.

Chapter 8
Sam Goes Exploring

Sophie and Grandpa were fastening their coats – the sun was shining, but there was a chilly wind even though it was late February. Sophie thought Sam should be wearing his new coat as well – she didn't want him to get a chill. She had to hold him tightly to stop him running around her legs as fast as he could.

'Sam, you are a very excited puppy! We're nearly ready, sit,' said Sophie, facing Sam. 'He was much better behaved at the class this morning.'

Grandpa laughed and bent down to hold Sam while Sophie clipped his lead on. He did look very smart.

'Okay, all ready now. Let's see if we can practise what we learned at the class. Remember, you are in charge Sophie, not Sam.'

'I know, if he runs on, I have to bring him

back and make him walk beside me,' said Sophie.

'Well remembered, that is exactly right,' said Grandpa.

Sophie opened the front door and Sam shot out, pulling on the lead, desperate to get to the gate. Sophie nearly fell over. 'Sam, sit,' she said. Sam sat down and looked straight at Sophie with big, excited eyes.

'Okay, let's go,' said Sophie.

'Woof,' said Sam, setting off again.

Sophie opened the gate and Sam shot off down the street, nearly knocking Sophie off her feet again. 'Sam,' she shouted. 'Sit.' Sam sat down again, looking at Sophie with big hopeful eyes.

'Let's try making his lead shorter so that he can't run so far. It'll be safer like that, so he can't run off the pavement. And you can keep him walking by your side until he calms down,' said Grandpa.

Sophie pulled the lead in and pressed the lock button on the handle so Sam was at her side.

'Good, he is just a puppy and he hasn't been out before, so we should expect him to be a bit excited. Remember to give him treats and praise when he behaves,' said Grandpa. 'Let's head to the park. He will have a lot of room to run about there safely.'

Sophie kept the treat bag in her right-hand pocket. 'Good boy, Sam,' she said regularly when she managed to keep him close as they walked to the park. Sophie noticed that he barked just once at everyone who passed them. People smiled because he was so cute. Sophie was beginning to feel a bit more confident.

It was a short walk to the park; she usually liked to stop at the gift shop and to look in the jeweller's window but today she thought it best to walk on.

'We made it!' she said. She enjoyed

coming to this park with Max and Harry and often met her friends here too. It had windy paths, bushes and trees and was good for playing hide and seek.

As she was looking for a bench for Grandpa to sit on, she met their neighbour Mrs Brown and her dog Juniper. 'Hello Sophie, is this your puppy?'

'Yes, it's his first walk and he's a bit excited,' said Sophie. Sam was running round Juniper, standing on two legs, sniffing and bouncing up and down as though he was on a spring. She hoped Juniper didn't mind – he seemed very patient and just let Sam run round him. Sam's lead was becoming all tangled round Juniper and Mrs Brown.

'He's just a puppy, you have to be kind but firm and he will be like Juniper soon,' laughed Mrs Brown as she untangled the lead.

'I hope so, we're going to puppy classes so that we can learn together and Grandpa's helping me,' said Sophie.

'That's a good idea. Maybe we'll see you again soon. Bye Sophie, bye Sam,' said Mrs Brown.

'Let's walk past the trees and up to the pond and you can stretch the lead right out and give Sam a bit of freedom,' said Grandpa.

Sophie made the lead longer and Sam ran on immediately. While he was running round bushes and sniffing, Sophie was watching all the other dog owners in the park. Their dogs all came back when they called. Sophie hoped Sam would do that too in a few weeks.

Today, he was darting everywhere, interested in absolutely everything – the flowers, the bushes, other dogs, the pond! 'No Sam, not in the pond, it's too cold for that,' said Sophie as she pulled him back. Grandpa was smiling as he sat on the seat, watching Sophie and Sam explore.

Suddenly, Sam started running quickly,

pulling Sophie along – she couldn't pull him back and just had to run as fast as he was. At first, Sophie couldn't see why Sam was running. Then she spotted a wee white fluffy tail speeding in front – a rabbit!

'Stop Sam, stop!' shouted Sophie.
Suddenly, the white tail disappeared and Sam stopped, looking all about him, a bit confused. Sophie laughed. She was out of breath. She shortened Sam's lead again and, as she walked back to Grandpa's bench, she saw her friends Emma and Hannah. She waved and they waved back and started walking towards her.

'Hello Sam,' said Hannah, tickling him as he jumped up, excited to see her.

'He's gorgeous, Soph, you are so lucky!' said Emma as she fussed over Sam. 'Can I take him on a wee walk to the next bench, Soph?' she asked.

'Of course, just keep a firm hold – he can

get a bit excited,' said Sophie, handing over the lead.

Sam wasn't too sure and kept looking back at Sophie, so Sophie walked with them. He was really good for a whole minute and then, as they turned round, he ran as fast as he could back to Grandpa, pulling Emma along behind him.

'Sam, Sam, slow down!' gasped Emma as she ran back and handed the lead to Grandpa who laughed.

'He's fast!' said Emma, sitting down on the bench.

'I know, he almost pulled me off my feet too when we first left the garden,' said Sophie. 'Do you want a shot Hannah?' she asked.

'Maybe next time, I'm going out with Mum and I promised not to be late home,' said Hannah as she tickled Sam.

'See you on Monday,' shouted Sophie as the girls headed off. Sophie went for another walk with Sam who kept running as far as his lead would allow!

What a lot of energy he had thought Sophie.

'I think Sam has had a lovely first walk and we should head home now, it won't be long until the light is going,' said Grandpa.

Sophie was feeling very pleased – Sam was walking much better at her side as they headed home and it was great to see Emma and Hannah. He was a clever puppy – she was sure he would be a good dog when he grew up.

Back on the main road, they walked past the bank. Almost home now, Sophie thought. As he walked round the big black litter bin, Sam gave a wee yelp. Sophie looked down. Oh no – lots of broken glass bottles were all around the other side of the bin and she hadn't noticed them. Now, she could see red spots on the pavement – blood.

'Grandpa,' shouted Sophie. 'I think Sam has hurt his paw on the broken glass.'

Grandpa stopped and picked Sam up. Sophie could see a piece of glass in his paw and it was pouring with blood.

'I think we need to call Dad,' Grandpa said. 'I'll keep holding Sam and you take my phone out of my pocket and ask Dad to pick us up as Sam has a wee injury. Tell him I don't want Sam to walk on his paw,' said Grandpa.

Sophie did as Grandpa asked and called Dad. 'Dad says he is just coming, Grandpa. I told him we are at the gift shop.'

'Good,' said Grandpa. 'Vandals – they are just so thoughtless. It's disgraceful!' Sophie could see that Grandpa was angry; she felt annoyed she hadn't noticed the glass.

Dad pulled up and looked at Sam's paw. 'Vet I think for this little one,' he said. 'I will call him now and let him know we need an emergency appointment. Sophie, can you hold Sam carefully? Take some tissues and dab the blood away but try not to touch the glass or it will hurt Sam.'

Sophie carefully cuddled Sam as tears began to roll down her cheeks – poor Sam. She could see Dad's face in the mirror and he looked worried. Sam seemed still and quiet which wasn't like him.

Dad pulled up at the vet's and Grandpa helped her out of the car. Sophie was grateful that there was no queue. Mr Smith the vet called them in right away.

'Hello Sophie, I didn't expect to see you and Sam so soon. What happened today?'

Sophie explained about the smashed bottles she hadn't seen and showed Mr Smith the piece of broken glass stuck in Sam's paw. It was still bleeding quite badly. She showed Mr Smith all the tissues with blood on them.

'Oh dear, poor Sam, this is a nasty cut and dogs' paws do bleed very badly. It can be really serious. It was good that Dad and Grandpa were quick to bring Sam in to see me.' Mr Smith brought in his assistant, Lucy, who helped hold Sam while he gave him an injection to numb his paw and another injection to make him a bit sleepy.

Tears were still running down Sophie's face. This was just awful – she couldn't believe it. Her beautiful puppy, hurt. Dad gave her a hug.

Mr Smith carefully examined Sam's paw and, using big tweezers, pulled the glass out. He inspected the paw with a magnifying glass for some time and then took some other little bits of glass out. Finally, he stitched Sam's paw.

'I think he is going to be just fine. He can't go for walks for about a week and you need to give him some antibiotics so that he doesn't get an infection. Bring him back in a week for me to check please Sophie.'

Sophie picked Sam up and gave him a big hug. 'I love you and I promise to look after you.'

'It's not your fault Sophie, the vandals are the ones to blame,' said Mr Smith.

'Thank you for helping Sam,' she said through her tears.

Dad picked up his medicine. Sophie cuddled Sam all the way back home. As she stroked his bandaged paw, she was so glad that Grandpa and Dad had known what to do. It might not be her fault but she would certainly be more careful in future. Sam was far too precious to be injured again.

Chapter 9
Sam Visits Aunty Claire

Sam's paw was now fully healed and his walks had been event free; Sophie looked carefully now for any glass that might be lying around.

She was feeling excited this morning as she watched Mum and Dad put their weekend cases in the car. Aunty Claire was looking after them for Easter while Mum and Dad went to Edinburgh. Sam hadn't stayed at Aunty Claire's house before. Sophie always looked forward to visits to her Aunty Claire but she was feeling a little nervous – Sam was always chewing shoes that he found lying around and she hoped he wouldn't find any nice shoes at Aunty Claire's house.

Last week, Harry had been furious at Sam – jumping up and down mad – when Dad said he had to buy new football boots with his piggybank money after Sam chewed his old pair. Sophie had told everyone not to leave anything lying about because Sam was at that chewing stage puppies go through but Harry had forgotten and left his football boots on the floor. Sophie had hoped Dad would help Harry buy the new football boots but Dad had said that Harry would remember better if he had to pay with his own money.

Sam had also chewed Gran's handbag strap, although Gran had said it was her own fault because she had left it on the floor. And Mum had a nice pair of blue work shoes chewed too. Surprisingly, Dad always said, 'Don't worry Sophie – you explained that Sam would be likely to chew things if he found them. Everyone needs to listen.' Mum was also kind about it. She explained to Sophie that babies chew things too – it is how they learn. She hoped the chewing stage would be over soon – it was hard work checking everyone was tidy.

Sophie put her overnight bag in the boot.

'Will I need to put a bag in for Sam too?'

'No need,' said Dad. 'Aunty Claire has bought a bed and some food bowls. Just take his lead and some chew toys.' Sophie already had the chew toys and the lead ready.

Aunty Claire was a good fun aunty and nothing was too much bother – swimming, museums, park visits, baking, the list was endless. She lived alone in a small two-bed terraced house, which had a very neat back garden with grass and a row of pretty flowers down one edge. According to Aunty Claire, 'It was just ideal for one aunt and her nieces and nephews to visit.' Sophie thought it was just perfect. The kind of house she would like to have when she was grown up.

She wondered what Aunty Claire had planned for this visit. It was the first time she'd had Sam to stay and, as it was Easter, Sophie knew that there would be some treats for everyone. Dad had given her a bag with a chocolate egg to give to Aunty Claire on Sunday. Sophie just knew that Sam would love her house.

'I'm ready,' said Harry, jumping up and down at the edge of the pavement.

'Stop jumping Harry and go and put your bag in the boot,' said Dad. 'Max, are you ready? Everyone else is waiting.'

'Just coming, I'm checking this is a good book for Aunty Claire to read to us,' said Max.

At last everyone settled into the car - Mum and Dad in the front, Sophie sitting with Harry and Max in the back seat. Sam was looking out of the window from his boot seat with his seatbelt fastened. Sophie put her hand over the back and Sam gave it a wee nudge.

Sam seemed to enjoy watching the trees blowing in the breeze and the new lambs running around the fields as they drove along. It was quite a short drive to Aunty Claire's. In no time at all, the car had stopped outside her house.

Sophie laughed – Aunty Claire was on the pavement waving frantically, bending down and sticking her hands through her legs and waving again. She was just as bouncy as Harry. Sophie, Harry and Max jumped out of the car and hugged Aunty Claire.

'Whoa,' she laughed.

'You're all getting taller, you'll knock me down soon. Where's the special new boy?'

'Right here,' said Sophie as she lifted the boot lid, unclipped his lead and an excited Sam jumped out, barking once as he usually did.

'Well, you've grown since Christmas Day,' said Aunty Claire, shaking Sam's paw as he held it out. 'Oh, what a lovely clever dog.'

Sam ran straight in through the front door. 'Well that's good – he knows where to go!' Everyone laughed and followed.

Sophie checked the hall floor for shoes or

handbags. None – Aunty Claire had thought of everything.

'Cookies and tea will be just perfect, thanks,' said Dad as Aunty Claire appeared with a tray of mugs and a plate of cookies. Mum and Dad enjoyed Aunty Claire's delicious cookies before they left.

'Well, what'll we do today?' asked Aunty Claire once everyone had waved goodbye to Mum and Dad. 'It's a nice sunny spring day – a good day for a walk in the park with Sam or we could walk along the promenade to the ice cream shop for some ice cream.'

'Promenade,' said Harry and Max together – they loved the ice cream shop, with its rows of delicious ice creams.

'Promenade it is, Sophie. I think Sam needs his lead on today, it's a new place, it'll be busy this weekend and he'll be a bit excited I expect,' said Aunty Claire picking up her phone and her jacket. 'Let's go. We're off for an ice-cream treat.'

Chapter 10
Clever Sam

Sophie liked walking along the promenade to the ice cream shop. It was a wide flat path and they all walked together. It was always a fun walk. Today, Aunty Claire was doing silly walks, first like a bear. Sophie laughed at her brothers as they joined in. Sam ran with Harry and back to Max, almost tripping Aunty Claire as he ran between her legs.

'I'm a snake,' said Harry, challenging them to wriggle along with Sam running alongside.

Sophie saw the queue at the ice cream shop right at the end of the promenade. On sunny days, it always had a queue – the ice cream was delicious and everyone wanted one. When they reached the café, Sophie sat on one of the chairs outside with Sam at her feet while Max, Harry and Aunty Claire went in to buy the ice creams. Sam strained on his lead, trying to see where they had All gone and hoping to go too. Sophie tried tickling his ears but he wasn't for settling.

In a few minutes, they reappeared carrying large cones in different colours. Sophie hoped hers was a chocolate one. She took the small white cone that Harry was carrying for Sam.

'Look at this Sam – a new treat, special dog ice cream,' she said.

He looked at it for a minute and then started licking the cone all round. He licked faster and faster as he enjoyed this new treat. Sophie had to hold it firmly so that Sam didn't pull it out of her hand. In no time at all, it was gone. He looked longingly at Sophie as she licked her ice cream.

'Absolutely not Sam, one ice cream is quite enough and mine isn't doggy ice cream.'

Ice creams eaten, they headed back along the prom. It was just as much fun as the walk to the ice cream shop. This time, Aunty Claire said, 'You have to walk very carefully with small steps just like this along the promenade without standing on any lines or cracks. If you stand on a crack or line, you have to hop for one minute.'

Harry of course just wanted to hop so he stood on lines all the time and Sam ran around his legs not sure why he was stopping and hopping.

'Come on Sam, Harry is okay, he just likes hopping,' said Sophie, pulling Sam's lead.

'It's good to know that Sam looks after everyone,' said Aunty Claire. 'Let's head down to the beach and we can skim stones into the water.'

They all ran down the slipway, Harry making it onto the beach first. At the start of the sand, Sam ran back and barked before sitting beside the large blue bins at the edge of the slipway.

'Come on Sam, you'll be fine on the beach. The sand's quite soft. Nothing to worry about,' said Sophie as she pulled on his lead.

Sam didn't seem to be listening though and He ran back to the bins, sat down again and barked looking at Sophie.

'Sam don't be silly,' said Sophie, picking him up. 'Sand's soft, you'll be fine.'

'Is Sam, okay?' asked Aunty Claire.

'He hasn't seen a beach before, I think he's just a bit unsure,' said Sophie.

'Perhaps he can have his lead off while we are on the beach. He might like that,' said Aunty Claire.

'Okay, I'll walk a little bit further so that he stays on the beach before I put him down,' said Sophie.

After a few more steps, Sam was beginning to feel a bit heavy and Sophie put him down carefully and unclipped his lead. Sam ran round her legs and just as she was laughing, she saw him run straight back to the bins at the slipway. Sophie ran as fast as she could to catch him.

'Sam, come back here at once!' shouted Sophie, feeling annoyed.

Sam ran straight back to the middle blue bin, sat down and barked. Thank goodness he'd stopped running Sophie thought, but she was still a bit annoyed.

'Sam, you'll just have to have your lead on, I'm not running back here all the time, I don't want to play at the bins. Come on, sand is fun,' she said.

As she bent down to put on Sam's lead, she noticed a small foot wearing a blue trainer sticking out from behind the bin. It looked very strange and she felt a little worried. She walked carefully round the bin and there she saw a small boy lying on the ground, not moving, and a small blue and white bicycle lying on the ground behind him. She stopped and stared and then quickly shouted, 'Aunty Claire, help! Help! You need to call an ambulance.'

Aunty Claire came running up and some other people on the beach came running over too.

'Look,' said Sophie. 'He isn't moving.'

A man wearing swimming shorts opened his phone.

'Can we have an ambulance please? There is a small boy unconscious on the beach.'

'Do you know him?' the man asked Sophie.

'No, my dog found him,' said Sophie.

Sophie heard the man say, 'No, no-one knows him at the moment.'

'Harry, Max, let's go up and down the beach asking if anyone has lost a small boy,' said Aunty Claire. Harry and Max followed her.

The ambulance and a police car arrived quickly and Sophie and the man in the shorts moved back to let them in. The small boy was still not moving.

'Hello,' said the ambulance driver as he gently touched the boy's arm. 'I'm Tom, I'm an ambulance driver and I've come to see if you are hurt. Can you hear me? What's your name?'

To everyone's relief, the boy's eyes slowly opened. 'Mark,' he said in a small whisper.

'Excellent Mark, it's good to chat to you, now, I'm going to check you over and you tell me if anything hurts, okay?'

Mark nodded. 'No broken bones. Is anything feeling sore?'

'My head,' said the small voice.

'Okay, we're going to put you on a stretcher and take you to hospital for a doctor to look at you. Do you know where your mum or dad are?' said the ambulance driver.

Just then, a lady came rushing down the slipway shouting, 'Mark, Mark, what happened to you? I thought you were behind me!'

'Are you Mum?' asked the ambulance driver.

'Yes, I thought he was cycling behind me. Is he okay?' she asked, kneeling down beside the boy.

'I think he will be okay, but he has hit his head. We'll take him to hospital to be checked,' said the ambulance driver.

Mark's mum looked quite shocked but nodded.

'You can come with us in the ambulance. Who found him?' asked the ambulance driver.

'Sam did,' said Sophie.

'Sam?' said the ambulance driver.

'Yes, I'm Sophie and Sam is my dog.'

The ambulance driver smiled. 'Well, can you tell that police officer all about it, Sophie?'

Sophie nodded and gave Sam a great big cuddle. What an afternoon!

'I think Sophie looks as though she's had a big fright,' said the kind police officer. 'What if I give you all a lift home and you can tell me all about it then?'

'A lift in a police car?' said Harry. 'This is a great afternoon!'

'Harry, a little boy has been hurt, it's not a great afternoon,' said Max.

'It's great to have a ride in a police car,' said Harry.

Sophie climbed into the back of the police

car with Harry and Max and Sam sat on her knee. Aunty Claire sat in the front and gave the police officer directions.

Sitting back in Aunty Claire's house, Sophie told the police officer about Sam running back to the bins and barking and she thought he was just being silly until she saw the boy's foot.

'Well, that's certainly a very clever dog you have there. Young Mark is very lucky Sam found him. And well done to you too Sophie, you called for adults and that was exactly the right thing to do.'

After the police officer left, Aunty Claire suggested they should have a quiet night playing board games. They could maybe bake some cakes tomorrow before Mum and Dad came back. Sophie was glad that everyone agreed – it had been an extraordinary day. Harry brought out Operation; he liked the buzzing noise and Sophie was sure he pretended to be clumsy on purpose.

Max won. Sophie was still feeling out of sorts – she hoped the wee boy would be okay.

Chapter 11
News to Tell

Next morning, Aunty Claire had the breakfast table all set with egg cups in each place, some fluffy chick decorations on the toast rack and mini eggs scattered on the table. The breakfast eggs were boiling in the pot on the stove.

'Yum,' said Harry, eating a chocolate mini egg as he sat down beside Max who was also munching one.

'Now,' said Aunty Claire, 'to find your big chocolate eggs, there is a clue on your table mat. The yellow trail is Sophie, the blue is Max and Harry you are red. Read the clue and it will take you to the next clue and fingers crossed you find your egg. The eggs are hidden high up so that Sam can't reach them –
remember, chocolate is poisonous for dogs so don't share,' warned Aunty Claire. 'Ready? Go!'

Nobody needed to be told twice – they all

ran off and Sam didn't know who to follow. The garden wasn't big but Aunty Claire had hidden them well.

'Found mine!' shouted Max as he held up a big Maltesers egg.

'Me too,' shouted Sophie and Harry as they held up theirs. They headed back in and Sam ran over to his bed and then back to Sophie with a bag of treats in his mouth. Everyone laughed.

'Come on Sam, I'll give you some,' said Sophie, putting four in his bed. Sam gobbled them up and looked at Sophie.

'Cheeky boy, no more,' said Sophie laughing.

'I wonder how Mark is?' Sophie said as they were eating breakfast.

'I expect he'll be fine,' said Aunty Claire. 'Sam was really clever to find him. And we thought he was just being silly.'

'I know. I don't know how he knows that

someone needs help. He did the same thing at Hogmanay when he found Colin crying in Harry's bedroom. We thought he was being silly then too, but he wasn't.'

'Some dogs do have an extremely good sense of smell and are able to sense or smell things we can't. A lot of dogs are trained to do special jobs.'

'Well, I'm glad that Sam is my special puppy. I don't want him to be trained for anything else.'

'Can they make you train your puppy for a special job?' asked Max, concerned.

'Not unless you are asked and you agree,' said Aunty Claire. 'Now, shall we do some baking for Mum and Dad?' she asked as she pulled open her baking drawer.

Max and Harry collected the butter and the eggs from the fridge and Sophie put the oven on. They always enjoyed baking with Aunty Claire –

she always had a lovely choice of toppings for the cupcakes; today, it was mini eggs, fluffy chicks and chocolate bunnies. Aunty Claire, like Gran, was good at baking.

They had just finished decorating the cakes when Harry shouted, 'Look – Mum, Dad!' as their car pulled up outside.

As they ran out to see Mum and Dad, Sophie noticed a blue car pulling up behind their car. To her surprise, Mark and his mum climbed out of the blue car. Mark was wearing a head bandage.

'Hello,' said Sophie. 'We were just wondering how you were.'

'Mark's doing very well, thanks to you and your dog Sam,' said his mum.

Mark held out a toy and a bag of treats. 'These are for Sam, to say thank you for finding me.'

Sam ran round Mark's legs and barked,

wagging his tail.

'I think he looks pleased,' laughed Sophie. 'Thank you.'

'Hello,' said Sophie's dad. 'Did Mum and I miss some excitement?'

'You certainly did. Sam was a very clever dog and Sophie was a very sensible girl. And I am a very proud aunty,' said Aunty Claire as she joined them on the pavement.

'I hope you don't mind Mark and me visiting; my next-door neighbour told me you were a receptionist at the medical centre and knew where you lived,' said Mark's mum.

'No problem, it's good to see Mark recovering. We were wondering how he was,' said Aunty Claire.

As they waved goodbye to Mark and his mum, Dad said, 'Let's have a cup of tea and you can tell Mum and me all about it. This is quite a special Easter day.'

'Can we have cake too?' asked Harry. Everyone laughed as they headed in for a scrumptious tea.

Chapter 12
Sam Goes To School

'Back to school tomorrow, time to pack bags and look out uniforms,' said Mum.

'Aw, do I have to?' said Harry. 'Sam and I were just going out to play football.'

Max got up to join them. 'Me too,' he said hopefully.

Sam stood up, his tail wagging at the mention of football. Sophie looked at Dad.

'No football, do as you're told,' said Dad.

The boys stomped off up the stairs, not too pleased but knowing it was no use arguing. Sam followed, racing past them on the stairs.

Sophie took Sam back downstairs and settled him into his bed. 'Oh Sam, I will miss you tomorrow when I go to school,' she said as she cuddled him. Sam gave her a wee kiss and snuggled in. It felt good to have him beside her, he felt just like a cosy blanket.

Morning walk over and having settled Sam down with his toys and a treat, Sophie left for school with Harry, Max and Victoria. First day back after the holidays always felt like a long day. Today though there had been some good news and she couldn't wait to go home and share it.

'Hi, Grandpa – good news!' said Sophie, not stopping to put her bag down or take off her coat. 'I've to do a personal talk at school and Mrs Johnstone says I can do it about looking after Sam. And best of all, she says Sam can visit the class,' she puffed, out of breath. It was a warm spring day and she had run home as quickly as she could; it was Grandpa's day for after school.

Grandpa laughed. 'Well, that's very special.'

'Can you help me Grandpa? I can do it in

PowerPoint for the Smartboard.'

'In PowerPoint for the Smartboard?' said Grandpa. 'What's a Smartboard?'

'It's a big whiteboard in the classroom that works with the computer – haven't you seen one?'

'No love, I haven't. They had blackboards and chalk when I was at school, and definitely no computers. I think it's Dad who needs to help you, not me,' said Grandpa.

'Oh, okay, I'll ask Mum and Dad,' she said.

'I'm sure they'll be a much better help than me or Gran. It's puppy class tonight – are we going out for a walk to practise the commands again before the class?'

'I'll go and get changed.'

'And have a snack before you go,' said Gran from the kitchen.

'Okay,' said Sophie, grabbing an apple from the fruit bowl. It was the second last puppy class and while Sam certainly wasn't perfect, at least he wasn't naughty like Angus. Poor Debbie had a terrible time every class, Angus just didn't seem to want to do what he was told. Sophie was glad she didn't have the naughty puppy. It was funny to watch Angus, he had such a lot of personality, he was a cheeky wee puppy. Sophie wondered what Dad would say if Sam was so naughty.

She would talk to Dad about her homework after puppy class.

'Ready?' asked Grandpa.

'Ready,' she said, fetching Sam who was trying to chase Harry with a ball in the garden. Now that he was a little bigger, she noticed that Harry didn't always win. Sam was becoming a footballer – well, he could head the ball and catch it in his mouth before it landed on the ground.

'What are we learning tonight?' asked Grandpa.

'Well, we're still practising sit, stand, wait,

come and walking on lead. And I think there will be more socialising with the other puppies. He's okay with all the other puppies in the class, but I think he likes Ben best. Tonight, we're talking about family rules and in a few weeks we'll see if he can pass his Bronze Award,' she said.

'Well, we'll keep practising on our walks. He's good most of the time and I don't think they expect bouncy puppies to be perfect. Don't worry.'

'Dad'll be really pleased if he passes,' she said, crossing her fingers.

'Mum, Dad!' shouted Sophie as she came back from the class. 'Hi you two,' said Dad. 'How was the class tonight?'

'Good most of the time,' she said. 'Sam wasn't walking so well – he likes Ben and they have wee chases with one another. Angus was behaving better tonight. But I've special news.'

'Special news?' said Mum from the kitchen.

'Yes, I've to do a personal talk in two weeks' time for the class and Mrs Johnstone says I can talk about looking after Sam. And she says he can visit the class if an adult can collect him when I am finished.'

'Well that's exciting. I think the class will like your talk,' said Mum.

'I might need some help to prepare a PowerPoint,' she said.

'No problem, either Dad or I can help with that,' said Mum. 'And maybe Grandpa can collect Sam?' she said, looking at Grandpa.

'Of course I can collect Sam, just let me know the day, love.'

Sophie was feeing excited – not only did she have a beautiful puppy, but she could also take him to school. How lucky! After she fed Sam, they both cuddled up on the sofa as she began to write a list of things to put in her talk. She would start working on it tomorrow night and keep practising until she was confident.

The next night after dinner she sat with Dad and they began to prepare her PowerPoint. Sophie got out her list from the previous night.

'What about this list?' she asked:

'My Surprise

Feeding

Grooming

Exercise

Playing

Puppy classes.'

'I can't think of anything else.'

'These seem like good choices,' said Dad. 'Now think of some short phrases as bullet points for each slide, to help you remember what to say.'

'Thanks Dad,' she said as she wandered into the kitchen to work at the table. Mum was making soup and it smelled delicious. 'Mum, will you listen to me every night to make sure I'm remembering all the important things?'

'Of course, you just let me know when,' said Mum.

'Can I listen too, Sophie?' asked Max. 'I'm good at remembering things.'

'Thanks Max.'

Today was Sophie's big day and she woke feeling very nervous but very excited. She was taking Sam to school with her! She checked that toys and treats were packed for him in her school bag. She had practised her talk every night and both Mum and Dad said she was good. Even Max said it was good. She hoped her classmates would think so too.

She could hardly eat any breakfast. It wasn't really the talk that was making her nervous. 'Mum, what'll I do if Sam misbehaves and won't do as I ask? He might be too excited with the whole class there.'

'I'm sure Mrs Johnstone will help if that happens, she's a nice teacher.'

'Yes, she is and she likes dogs, she has one too.'

'If you are calm, Sam will be calm too. I'm sure it'll be fine. He is a puppy – no-one expects him to be perfect.'

Sophie thought Mum was probably right; she crossed her fingers and hoped. There were a couple of girls in the class who weren't always so nice and she could just imagine what they would say if Sam was silly. 'Maybe Sam needs more classes, Sophie' or 'Don't worry Sophie, he might be a good dog one day.' It was the way Chloe and Ella said things which was unkind, it made it difficult to tell a teacher, without sounding dramatic.

After putting her bag and jacket on, Sophie clipped on Sam's lead. Mrs Johnstone had told her to come to the front door this morning with Sam and not to line up at the classroom door in case he became too excited. She practised 'sit', 'wait', 'stand' and 'let's go' all the way to school. So far, Sam was having a good morning. She was feeling a little calmer by the time she reached the school gates.

As Sophie pressed the bell at the front door, she saw Mrs Johnstone waiting for her through the glass.

'Hello Sophie, what a lovely puppy you have,' said Mrs Johnstone as she let them in. Sam as usual barked once and ran round Mrs Johnstone's legs. Mrs Butler in the office laughed and came out to speak to him.

'Now Sophie, I think you should unpack your things and I'll hang up your coat and bag. You could sit in the hall until I have settled the class and then we'll have your talk. Who's picking Sam up?' asked Mrs Johnstone.

'My grandpa,' said Sophie.

'Excellent. Mrs Butler, can you call him please when Sophie has finished her talk?'

'Of course. Sophie can wait in the office with me until her grandpa arrives, I love dogs and he is so cute.' Sophie smiled at Mrs Butler.

She waited in the hall as Mrs Johnstone suggested and cuddled Sam. She whispered, 'Sam please be a good puppy, I love you so much and I want everyone else to love you too.' Sam cuddled in but Sophie could feel he was excited.

'Please Sam, be good.'

She saw Mrs Johnstone waving to her from the classroom door. 'Ready Sophie?'

She picked up her bag of things to show the class and kept Sam on a short lead. 'Let's go,' she said, feeling a bit nervous. 'I hope he behaves,' she said to Mrs Johnstone as she reached the classroom.

'Sophie, he's a delightful puppy, don't worry,' said Mrs Johnstone kindly.

As she entered the class, she heard shouts of 'oh, he's so lovely', 'he's cute, what's his name?' and Sam barked his usual 'hello'. He was pulling on his lead – she was sure he wanted to run around.

'Okay everyone, settle down please,' came Mrs Johnstone's voice from behind. The class began to settle. 'Now, Sam is just a puppy and we don't want to frighten him so you need to be quiet.' The class slowly quietened and Sophie was grateful for Mrs Johnstone's help.

'Now Sophie, I think you should lengthen the lead a little and walk round the class so everyone who wants to can pat him. Sam can see everyone and then we will do your talk.'

She did as Mrs Johnstone suggested and walked Sam round the whole class. Sam jumped with his front paws out from one person to the next – he even managed to jump onto Emma's knee. She lifted him down and eventually everyone who wanted to pat him had been able to. Sam seemed more settled too, or maybe he was a bit tired from all the attention.

Mrs Johnstone sat at the front and she sat Sam beside her. 'Okay Sophie, I'll look after Sam while you do your talk.' Sophie smiled – Mum had been right, Mrs Johnstone was a good help.

Sophie touched the keyboard and her presentation came up. Sam seemed settled so she took a deep breath, looked at the class and began.

She put up a slide showing a picture of a shooting star, a Christmas tree and a snowman and explained about her wish. She noticed that everyone was quiet and listening. Her next slide said 'Christmas Surprises'.

She showed them the note she had found in the box and the photo of her and Sam in the garden that her Dad had taken. 'Oh, he's lovely,' she heard from Hannah. She smiled.

Sophie was beginning to feel more confident and started to take Sam's things out of the bag. 'This is his food and his bowl. And this is his brush, would anyone like to give him a brush?' Elias's hand shot up. Sophie gave him the brush and Sam rolled onto his back for Elias to brush his tummy. The class laughed. She showed them his toothbrush and his dental sticks.

Next, she explained about the puppy classes and that she hoped he would pass his Bronze Award next week. She took Sam from Mrs

Johnstone and said, 'These are some of the things he needs to do to pass his award. Sit,' she said. Sam sat and she gave him a treat. She moved to the side and said 'Stand' and Sam stood. The class all clapped and Sophie felt butterflies in her tummy – she was so proud of Sam. She smiled and gave him back to Mrs Johnstone.

Her last slide was a picture of Harry playing football with Sam. Everyone laughed. She explained that her brothers loved Sam too and Sam loved them.

At the end of the talk, the class clapped and Sophie felt her face go a little pink. It had been a good talk and she felt pleased with herself and Sam. 'Has anyone got a question?' she asked. Lots of hands went up.

'Okay, I think we will have just four questions so that Sophie can give Sam to her grandpa and he can go home,' said Mrs Johnstone.

'What's his longest walk?' asked James.

'A puppy has to build up the length of his walks. At the moment his longest walk is to the park,' said Sophie.

'What's the cheekiest thing he has done?' asked Omar.

'Probably chewing Harry's football boots! Harry wasn't pleased but he did know not to leave them lying around. He forgot and Sam found them.'

'Does he do anything clever?' asked Chloe.

'Yes, he seems to be good at noticing when someone is in trouble. He found a friend crying and he also found a little boy who had fallen off his bike at the beach,' she said.

'Has he been to the vet?' asked Gillian.

'Yes, twice,' said Sophie. 'Once to get his injections and the second time because he cut his paw on broken bottles smashed by vandals at the black bin beside the bank.'

'Did he need stitches?' Ella asked.

'Yes, I was very frightened because he lost a lot of blood,' said Sophie. She noticed that the class was quiet and listening carefully.

'That is an extremely sad story Sophie, I am sorry to hear that happened to Sam,' said Mrs Johnstone. 'It's good to see he has recovered. I think we should give Sophie and Sam another round of applause for a wonderful talk.' Sophie smiled.

'Bye Sam,' was all she could hear from lots of voices as she left the classroom.

'Good boy Sam,' she said as she gave him a well-earned snack and a cuddle and headed to the office to see Mrs Butler.

'Success?' asked Mrs Butler.

'Yes. They all liked Sam. And Mrs Johnstone was a big help,' said Sophie. She only had two more months in Primary Six and then she would be going into Primary Seven, her last year

In primary school – she would miss Mrs Johnstone, she was so kind.

Chapter 13
Secrets

Sophie rushed through the front door with Sam. 'Mum, Dad, Gran – guess what!' she shouted.

Mum smiled. 'Does that big smile tell me Sam passed?'

'Yes,' she said, waving Sam's Bronze Award certificate about. 'He's such a clever dog, he did everything first time.'

'He certainly did,' said Grandpa.

'Well done,' said Dad from behind his newspaper. Sophie hugged him.

Sam sat right at Dad's feet and he laughed. 'Well done Sam, you are a clever boy,' said Dad, patting him. Wagging his tail, Sam ran off into the back garden. Sophie felt a little glow of happiness all around her. That night, she packed Sam's certificate into her schoolbag, hoping she could have a quiet word with Mrs Johnstone the next day to share her news. Maybe Mrs Johnstone would tell the class. She didn't want to say anything herself in case it sounded like showing off – she didn't want to be like Chloe and Ella. Though so far, they hadn't said anything nasty to her about Sam.

It felt good that she had such a special bond with Sam.

Sophie suddenly realised that Sam had been in the garden on his own for a while. I should check on him and bring him back in, she thought. As she walked through the kitchen and looked out into the back garden, she couldn't see Sam. That's strange, she thought, where could he be?

Feeling quite puzzled, she stepped out of the kitchen and onto the first step. She was about to shout for him when she heard crying at the end of the garden. She stopped and listened; it seemed to be coming from under the table on the patio.

'Sam, they're always nasty, they call me

names, won't let me play and I don't know how to stop them. Oh Sam, what'll I do?'

Sophie was shocked. Sam seemed to be sitting under the table with Victoria who was crying.

Sophie went back into the kitchen and thought for a minute before coming back out, shouting, 'Sam, where are you?' She didn't want Victoria to know she had been listening.

'Sophie, Sam is over here with me,' shouted Victoria.

She noticed Victoria's red eyes.

'Oh there you are, I didn't see you two hiding under the table,' she said.

'He's been really kind to me,' said Victoria as Sophie joined them under the table. 'I hurt my knee.'

'What did you do to your knee, will I get your mum? It must hurt, you are usually so brave,' she said.

'I'm all better now I've had a cuddle with Sam.'

'Let me see your knee,' Sophie said, checking both knees. 'Are you sure it's your knee that's sore Victoria?'

Victoria began to cry again. Sophie sat next to her and Sam cuddled in between them. She tickled his ears.

'What's wrong, Victoria?'

Victoria sniffed. 'Some girls in my class won't let me play. They call me names and I don't know what to do. I think I might need a new school.'

'They're not nice girls Victoria, and you don't need a new school. They need to stop their bullying,' Sophie said. 'What are they saying?'

Victoria started to cry again. Between her sobs, Sophie heard, 'They say that I'm stupid because I'm dyslexic and struggle with my reading and writing.'

Sophie felt her face going red with anger. 'Really,' she said. 'That's disgusting, they are nasty girls. We need to tell. Does your mum know?'

'Don't tell my mum Sophie, it will just make it worse. I've tried to practise my reading every night, but it is so hard.'

'I am really angry Victoria and I think we need to tell an adult.'

Victoria looked so upset. Sophie knew she should tell someone; she didn't know what to do.

'Why don't you want to tell your mum?' she asked.

Victoria started crying again and Sam cuddled in even closer. 'I don't want you to tell, will you promise not to tell?'

'I can't promise that, Victoria. Bullying is not allowed at school. These girls are not allowed to say these things and they need to change their behaviour. It's wrong. Please tell me their names.'

'Gemma and Kirsty,' said Victoria between her sobs.

Sophie knew that their headteacher Mrs Hamilton would not be pleased to hear the story. She was always talking at assemblies about bullying being unacceptable and to tell an adult. She didn't want Victoria to cry anymore.

'I really do think you need to tell your mum. I'll come and speak to you in the playground tomorrow. I'll walk with you right up to your class line and not just into the playground.'

Victoria nodded. 'Okay, I'll tell Mum.'

Sophie wasn't too sure she was going to tell her mum but she didn't know what else she could do.

'Okay Sam, bedtime for you,' she said as she scrambled back up. She opened the joining gate for Victoria and gave her a hug. 'Remember, these girls are not nice, it's not you. Tell your mum.'

Victoria nodded.

'I'll see you in the morning,' said Sophie.

'Bye Sophie, bye Sam,' Victoria said, blowing him a wee kiss.

Sophie cuddled Sam. 'You are such a kind, clever dog.' Sam looked at her with his big eyes and then ran round the garden, looking back at her to chase him. 'Sam,' she laughed, running after him and throwing a ball which he caught before it hit the ground.

Sophie looked over the fence at Victoria's bedroom and saw that the light was on. She hoped she was telling her mum.

The next morning, she waited at Victoria's gate for her as usual. 'Hi Victoria,' said Sophie as Victoria appeared. They set off for school together.

'How was your talk with your mum last night?' asked Sophie as Max and Harry walked in front.

'Mum was really busy, so I didn't want to bother her. I'll talk to her tonight,' said Victoria. 'Sam's so lovely, Sophie, I wish I had a puppy like him,' she said, changing the subject.

Sophie wondered what she should do. She knew it was wrong to keep secrets like this but she did understand that Victoria might be frightened of the girls in the class. 'You need to tell an adult, Victoria. I'll help you if you want,' she said. Victoria didn't answer.

As they reached the school gates, Victoria said, 'Thanks for walking with me, Sophie. I'll go to my class line now. See you later.'

Sophie watched as Victoria ran up and stood at the back of the class line on her own. The other children were all chatting and some boys were pulling one another's bags but no-one spoke to Victoria. Sophie walked over to talk to Victoria for a few minutes before she went to find her own friends. She was worried, it wasn't nice.

At morning break, she found Victoria playing on her own. 'Hi Victoria, shall we go and play with some of the other children?'

'I don't think they'll play with me Sophie. Gemma and Kirsty will be cross with them if they do.'

Sophie wasn't sure what to do and stayed to chat to her for a while. When the bell rang she went back to her own friends.

'Is Victoria okay, Sophie?' asked Emma.

'She's having a difficult time with some of the girls in her class,' said Sophie.

'Has she told her mum?'

Sophie was pleased to have someone to talk to and told Emma the story.

'That's awful, Sophie, you need to tell an adult.'

'I know but I don't know how to do it and not make things worse for Victoria,' said Sophie.

'Sophie, to beat bullies you have to tell. If it's a secret then they can do and say what they like and no-one knows what they're doing.'

Sophie sighed. She knew that Emma was right, but she was worried that things could get worse.

'I will make sure her mum knows tonight,' she said.

Sophie found it hard to concentrate when she went back into class after break. She was relieved when the lunchtime bell rang. She knew that Victoria's year group was always the first lunch sitting so she decided to try and catch her once she'd had her lunch.

As she was clearing her desk, Mrs Johnstone came over to her. 'Sophie, are you okay? You seem to be a bit out of sorts today. Is Sam okay?'

'Sam's good,' she said. 'I'm just a bit worried about the little girl who lives next door to me who is in primary two.'

'Well, if you would like to talk to me, I'm here,' said Mrs Johnstone.

Sophie thought for a minute. 'It's actually about school and some people not being kind.'

'I think you should tell me, Sophie, and we can see what can be done about it. Everyone should feel safe at school and if you know something is wrong, you should share.'

'That's what Emma said, but I'm worried I'll make it worse for her.'

'Sometimes unkind people are annoyed when they are found out but if you and your next-door neighbour keep talking to us, we will stop it. Children usually want to be kind. The teachers normally find they can stop the problem quickly once they know about it,' said Mrs Johnstone.

Sophie sat down and told Mrs Johnstone the story she had told Emma. Mrs Johnstone listened carefully and Sophie saw her smile disappear. 'Sophie, this is bullying and I am very glad you shared it with me. Thank you for being so brave. We need to deal with this but don't worry – no teacher will say where the information came from.'

'Will I still keep an eye on Victoria?' she asked.

'If you want to chat to Victoria, of course you can, but the staff will start dealing with this today. And if you think there are any other problems in the future, please let me know.'

Sophie nodded, feeling relieved that an adult knew.

'Will I tell her mum tonight?' she asked. 'I don't think Victoria wants to.'

'Mrs Hamilton will talk to Victoria's mum today,' said Mrs Johnstone.

Sophie went for lunch feeling a lot better now that she knew that the teachers were helping to sort this. She really hoped it would be okay. Mrs

Hamilton was a kind headteacher, but she could also be strict if you weren't behaving. Sophie hoped she would stop Gemma and Kirsty being unkind to Victoria.

She went to find Victoria at the end of the day; to her surprise, she was chatting to two other girls in her class. 'Bye Victoria, see you tomorrow,' said one of the girls.

'She seems like a nice girl,' Sophie said to Victoria.

'Yes, she is. But guess what happened this afternoon,' Victoria said.

'I can't guess, tell me,' she said. 'Was it good?'

'Oh yes, Miss Potter talked to the whole class about being nice and playing nicely. And some girls told her about Gemma and Kirsty calling me names. Miss Potter wasn't happy and Gemma and Kirsty aren't allowed playtimes for a whole week.'

'Well, that's really great, Victoria.' Sophie felt a big worry cloud lifting and floating away.

'I know! And the other girls are talking to me now,' Victoria said with a smile. 'Miss Potter said the play leaders will help us play until the summer holidays. And Mrs Hamilton took Gemma and Kirsty out of the class,' Victoria laughed. 'They said sorry to me when they came back.'

The two girls played silly walks together as they walked home and Sophie thought how lucky she was to be in such a caring school. She needn't have worried, but she would let the teachers know if the bullying started again.

As they turned the corner, they saw Victoria's mum walking towards them. She wasn't usually home at this time. She knows, thought Sophie.

Chapter 14
Fun at St Andrews

As she jumped out of bed and pulled the curtains back, Sophie realised there was no need to be up at 7.30 – it was the first day of the summer holidays. Six weeks of freedom and walks with Sam.

She leapt back into bed, pulling her duvet up. She smiled as her door opened just a little bit. 'C'mon Sam,' she whispered and Sam rushed in, not needing a second telling, jumping straight onto Sophie's bed. 'Don't let Dad see you up here,' she laughed as they cuddled in together.

'Sophie, are you up? Sam needs a good walk before we go this morning. I can't see him,' Dad shouted upstairs.

'I'm up and getting dressed,' said Sophie, diving out of bed and gently pushing Sam back onto the stairs, before tiptoeing back into her room.

After their walk and breakfast, Sophie went outside to find Dad. 'Are my things in the car?' she asked.

'Yes, your bag and Sam's too,' said Dad. 'Strap Sam in please, Sophie, he needs to be safe. Right, is everyone in? Let's go,' said Dad.

'We're off!' shouted Harry and Sam looked at him with one eye open. 'Sorry Sam, I forgot you were snoozing.' Sophie smiled.

The two-hour drive to St Andrews passed quickly. Sophie knew it wasn't so far to go when they crossed over the new bridge at Queensferry; it stood in a row with the old Forth Bridge and the railway bridge. They always made Sophie feel quite special, sort of important. Three strong bridges standing in a row, one white and modern, one grey and tired looking and the red one made of steel for the trains. It just had to be a special place to need three bridges built over so many years. They connected the capital city Edinburgh to the

Kingdom of Fife. Just another forty minutes and they would be at the caravan park, ready to start their holidays. Sophie settled down to watch the green fields through her side window.

It wasn't too long before she patted Harry's arm to wake him. 'Wakey, wakey, sleepy head,' said Sophie.

'Are we here?' said Harry, rubbing his eyes. 'Wow, that didn't take long. Can I go to the park?'

'Jobs first,' said Mum. 'The car needs to be emptied. Put everything away and then you can go to the park.'

Sophie watched Harry dragging his bag along.

'Come on Harry,' said Max, giving his arm a punch as he passed. 'Bet I can put all my stuff away faster than you,' he said, picking up his bag and running in.

'Nope, I'll be first,' said Harry, running after him. Sophie laughed. Max was really clever sometimes – Harry liked games, especially when he might win.

Harry and Max had unpacked in record time and were ready to go to the park.

'I hope you two haven't just stuffed everything into the drawers,' said Mum.

'Course not,' said Max.

'Hmm! Well, enjoy the park,' said Mum. Sophie helped Mum unpack the food shopping. 'it's nice to have a helper. We'll join Dad and the boys at the park in a minute.'

Sophie passed her bedroom and saw Sam snoozing on the spare bed. He looked very settled.

'I think the swing park might be a bit dangerous for Sam,' Sophie said. 'There isn't much green space for him to run about.'

'That's true. It's a lovely day, why don't you and Sam head down the path to the beach and I'll see if I can persuade the boys to come down too,' said Mum.

Sophie fetched Sam, his lead and some treats and they made their way to the beach path. Sophie could smell the sea air and felt it going deep into her lungs as she breathed it in. It was a lovely familiar feeling, a special place to be. Sam was pulling on the lead, and she suddenly found herself running quickly down the path. He could probably smell the sea too she thought. He just loved the water.

The beach was unusually quiet today and Sophie was pleased. She unclipped the lead. As she stood up, she saw Sam running towards another dog. Oh no, she thought, running after him, he's so excited. Her sandals were keeping her back so she kicked them off, it was easier to run in her bare feet.

As she got closer, she smiled in amazement – she could see why Sam was so excited. 'Tom!' she shouted and Tom turned and waved as Ben came running towards her.

'Hi Sophie, Ben and Sam seem to have remembered one another,' he said, laughing as the two dogs jumped on one another in puppy fun.

'Yea, they liked one another at the puppy classes. Are you on holiday?' Sophie asked as she watched Ben and Sam running in and out of the little white frothy waves dancing on the sand.

'I'm up at the caravan park,' he said, pointing up the hill.

'So am I – we're at my gran and grandpa's caravan this week and next,' said Sophie.

'My mum and dad are renting a caravan and we're here for two weeks too.'

'Great, maybe we can walk Ben and Sam together sometimes, they would like that,' said Sophie.

'Sure,' said Tom.

'Hi Sophie, does Sam have a new friend?' asked Dad as he joined them.

'Oh, hi Dad, I didn't realise you were here

already. This is Ben and Tom – Grandpa and I met them at puppy classes.'

'I remember you telling me. Hello Tom,' said Dad. 'Look at these two, don't they just love the water,' said Dad laughing.

Sophie ran to join them. As she looked up, she saw that Dad had his shoes in his hand and was running into the water to splash with Sam and Ben too. Harry and Max were pulling off their trainers and socks too. It was a whole family splash.

It was a lovely afternoon, the perfect start to a holiday, blue skies and a warm sun beating down on them. Tom and Ben joined in and played fetch with a ball. Sam and Ben weren't too sure which ball to chase as they pushed one another out of the way.

'I'm off back to the caravan Sophie,see you and Sam tomorrow,' said Tom, waving as he left with Ben who kept looking back at Sam.

Exhausted, Sophie lay down on a towel to dry off as she watched Max, Harry and Sam all dig a big hole in the sand. She wasn't sure Sam was much help, but Harry and Max didn't seem to mind. He was making sand fly between his back legs and Harry and Max had moved out of the line of fire to the other side of the hole. Sophie watched her brothers move as Sam worked his way round the hole.

'I think we'll have a treat and have tea at the café tonight,' said Dad. Everyone agreed it was time up at the beach and began to pack up, drying their feet to put shoes and socks on to go up the path. As they headed back, Sophie noticed Sam wasn't running up the hill as quickly as he'd run down it earlier. He went straight into his bed when they arrived back at the caravan.

'Are you tired, Sam?' she said. 'I'm going to have my shower and change for tea while you have a snooze.' In no time at all, Sam was sound asleep. Sophie could imagine Gran saying, 'It's the sea air, it makes you sleep well.'

Tea at the café was delicious and her tummy felt full after her cheeseburger, chips and ice cream. Sam had enjoyed his special ice cream too.

As they walked back to the caravan, they passed Tom's caravan and Sam pulled on his lead, trying to go up the steps. Sophie smiled as Tom opened the door.

'Hi Sam, are you checking if Ben's coming out to play?' he said as Ben ran out to see Sam. Max and Harry ran over, delighted to have two dogs to play with, one each.

'C'mon Sam, time for bed, you will see Ben in the morning,' said Sophie as she pulled Sam away. Tom picked Ben up and carried him back into the caravan, waving his paw as they left.

'Bye Ben,' said Harry. 'Sophie, can I go for morning walks with you and Tom?'

'No Harry, it's enough for Sophie and Tom to look after two dogs, brothers as well is too much,' said Mum. 'You can play with Ben when he comes for Sophie and Sam in the mornings, if you're not still in your pyjamas.'

'Not fair,' said Harry, stomping off in a huff. Max laughed and Harry gave him a punch.

'Enough you two, don't spoil a nice day. It's almost bedtime,' said Mum.

As Sophie lay in bed that night, she thought about all the fun things she enjoyed at St Andrews: putting at the Himalayas putting green, swimming in the sea and at the pool, the trampolines at East Sands, exploring the old castle, shopping in all the lovely gift shops, tickling the fish at the aquarium, walks on the coastal path and now, best of all, splashing in the sea and digging in the sand with Sam. She wondered what Tom and Ben liked to do. Her thoughts drifted as she heard her family shouting, 'Goodnight.' She turned to Sam, but he was fast asleep in his bed and she closed her eyes too.

'Bacon rolls for breakfast today,' said Mum as she put a large plate in the middle of the table. There was a knock at the door and Sam was straight there. Sophie grabbed two rolls, one for her and one for Tom, and picked up Sam's lead and some treats.

'Just off for my walk with Tom and Ben, we'll be back in an hour,' she said.

'Not any longer please,' said Mum, handing her the poo bags which she put in her pocket.

'Hi Tom,' she said, handing him a bacon roll and clipping on Sam's lead. 'Coastal path or beach?'

'Coastal path to the cathedral. I have to be back in time for going to Craigtoun Park today and I don't want Ben all wet or to be late. Dad'll be annoyed if he makes the seats in the car wet,' said Tom.

'Oh my dad gets annoyed at that too,' said Sophie as she munched her bacon roll. 'Look at these two, play fighting and chasing.' Sam was loving having a friend and she thought that Ben was too.

They talked all the way to the old castle ruins while the dogs chased and ran. It was a walk along a proper path and up a hill to the ruins and the cemetery and this morning it was quiet. People had obviously been buried at the cathedral cemetery a long time ago. Some of the headstones were fenced off and being repaired. Sophie and Tom tried hiding behind some of the cemetery's ruined walls, but Ben and Sam were not to be fooled and found them every time.

It didn't take long to arrive back at the caravan park. The puppies were quick walkers especially when they chased one another. 'Bye Sophie, see you and Sam in the morning,' said

Tom.

'Bye Tom, enjoy the park,' said Sophie, catching Sam before he disappeared with Tom and Ben.

St Andrews

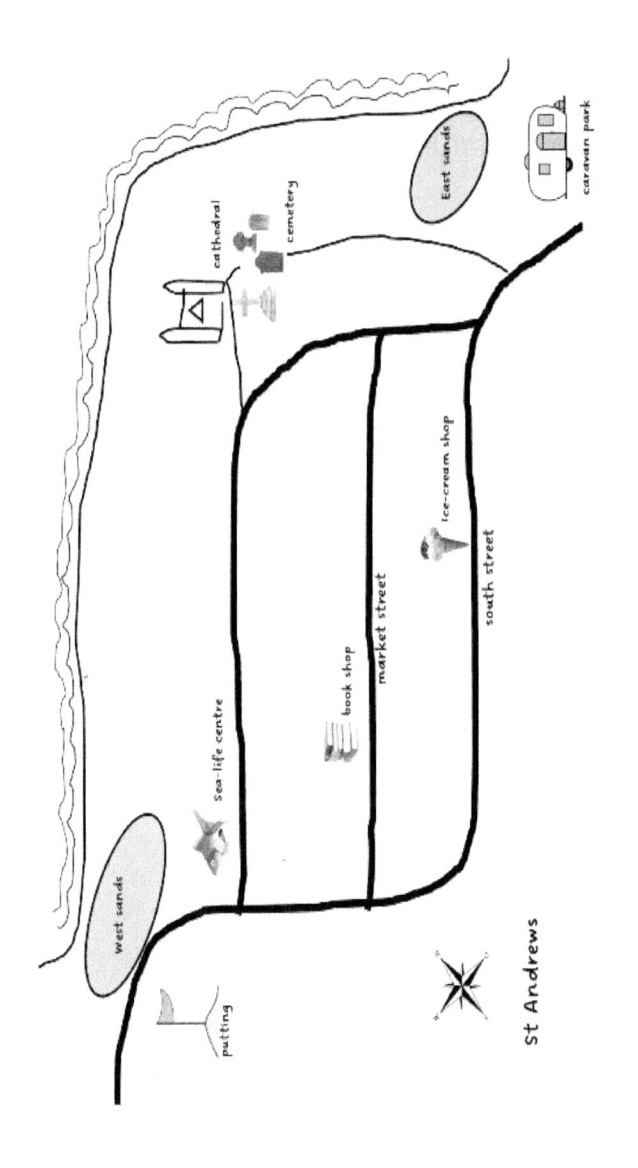

Chapter 15
On The News

Sophie looked forward to their morning walks. She loved the smell of the salty air and the pink and red skies as the sun climbed slowly into the sky above the sea.

Each day, they either went down onto the beach or they walked along the shore to the old castle and wandered round the cemetery. Sam and Ben loved the beach; they didn't do much swimming, just paddling and chasing one another in and out of the waves. The white frothy edges of the waves fascinated them; it was funny watching them trying to catch them. They never seemed to tire of that game, just happy to be in one another's company.

Sometimes they did a bit of digging in the sand. Ben was a better digger than Sam, his holes were much deeper. Sam seemed to just spread the sand about and pity help anyone standing behind him as sand flew around in no particular direction.

On cathedral and cemetery days, Tom and Sophie read the old headstones. They had to make sure the dogs didn't pee on the headstones, that didn't seem respectful. Sam and Ben were learning but they were both puppies and it was embarrassing sometimes, especially if other people were there.

Sophie was enjoying her first holiday with Sam. She hadn't gone on an aeroplane to a sunny place like some of her friends, but she'd had some great walks with Tom and Ben and she loved visiting all her favourite places in St Andrews. The coastal walks were perfect for exploring with Sam and her brothers who loved searching for crabs in all the little rockpools. Sophie had collected some very pretty shells on the beach which she would wash and take home. Victoria and Emma would like them.

Today was the second last day of the holiday and, as it was to be a sunny day, Mum and Dad and her brothers were going to join her for a beach day. She was heading out with Tom and Ben while everyone else was getting ready.

She heard Sam bark 'hello' to Ben and knew that Tom was at the door before he knocked. She picked up two bacon rolls, her beach bag for later and Sam's lead.

'Hi Tom, we're ready. I'm off Mum, see you later!' she shouted as she closed the door and gave Tom his bacon roll.

'Tomorrow's our last day at the caravan,' said Tom as they walked down the path. 'Ben has loved playing with Sam and being at the beach. He'll be lonely when we get home.'

'Sam will be lonely too. Maybe we can meet sometimes in the park at home so they can play together,' said Sophie.

'That would be great. I'll text you when I'm

going,' said Tom.

'Oh, I haven't got a phone, but you can call the house phone,' said Sophie.

They watched as Ben and Sam, now on the beach and lead-free, played their usual chasing game in and out of the waves. Tired of the waves, they moved to the soft sand.

'Ben's really much better at digging than Sam,' said Sophie as she watched them.

'Sam's just messy, he doesn't really make much of a hole.'

Just then, Ben, who had almost disappeared down the hole, gave a yelp and jumped back out of the hole, landing on all four paws. Sam moved forward and looked into the hole; he too yelped and jumped back onto his four paws.

Sophie laughed. 'Do you think they have found a crab and it's bitten their nose?'

Tom laughed. 'Probably,' he said as they

walked to the hole for a look. Tom peered in.

'It's not a crab,' he said. 'It's metal and has a sharp-looking bit sticking out.'

Sophie moved forward and Tom looked a bit serious. 'Let's put Sam and Ben on their leads,' he said. 'I've just been learning about World War 2 at school and I've seen a picture of that in one of the books. It looks like a grenade.'

'Really? Will it explode?' said Sophie, moving back quickly with Sam.

'I don't know. I think we should call the police,' said Tom.

'I'll go and get my dad,' said Sophie.

Tom fished his mobile phone out of his pocket and Sophie noticed his hands were shaking. He handed Ben's lead to Sophie.

'I can call the police and my dad,' said Tom as he started dialling 999.

Sophie watched in disbelief – a grenade, was that like a bomb? She followed Tom away from the hole. How did it get there?

'Hello, I think my dog may have found a World War 2 grenade buried in the sand,' said Tom. He listened while Sophie held on to Sam's and Ben's leads. 'We are at East Sands beach in St Andrews, below the caravan park.' Tom listened again. 'No, we are the only ones on the beach.' Tom was listening again. 'Okay, we can do that,' he said. He ended the call.

'What have we to do?' asked Sophie, not feeling safe.

'We have to move far away but stay on the path so that we can show the police where the hole is. They are sending someone over now,' said Tom.

Sophie followed Tom to the rocks at the edge of the beach, pulling Sam and Ben along, and sat down.

'I'm going to call my dad and he can let your dad know too,' said Tom.

Sophie nodded. She was feeling frightened and hoped the police would arrive soon. Just as Tom finished speaking to his dad, two police officers arrived on bikes. As they got closer, they jumped off their bikes and pushed them over towards Tom and Sophie.

'Hello, are you the two who think you found a grenade?' asked the taller officer.

'Yes, it's over there,' said Tom, pointing to the hole made by Ben and Sam. Sophie stayed with Tom and the dogs as the police officers inspected the hole. It wasn't long before they were back beside them.

'Well spotted! Strange that it is buried so deep, it must have come in on the tide a while ago to be that deep. We think it needs to be investigated, and we are going to close the beach off,' said one of the officers.

'What will happen now?' said Tom

'The bomb squad will come and check it,'

said the taller officer.

'Can we watch?' asked Tom.

'Well maybe if you go back further onto the big rocks over there. We'll see what the bomb squad say when they arrive, they shouldn't be long.'

Sophie could see her dad and Tom's dad walking down the beach path together and she felt relieved. It was all a bit worrying to find a grenade and speak to police officers and bomb squads. The police had put blue and white tape across the top of the beach path to stop anyone coming down.

'Did you really find a grenade?' asked Tom's dad.

'Maybe. The bomb squad are coming to check it. Ben was digging a big hole and found it,' said Sophie. 'Will it explode? I don't want Sam to get a fright.'

'it could explode, they can be unstable but

it's unlikely to,' said Tom's dad. 'The bomb squad will be coming from Leuchars Air Base.'

'I asked if we could watch and they said maybe from over here, but we need to see what the bomb squad say,' said Tom.

'Good job you two,' said Tom's dad.

'Sophie, do you want to go back to the caravan with Sam?' asked her dad just as a big blue truck with 'BOMB DISPOSAL UNIT' on the side arrived.

'Can I see what they say first?' asked Sophie, beginning to feel a bit braver. She could see the police officers talking to the team from the bomb disposal unit. They all put on vests and visors and helmets and then they all went to have a look at the hole.

Huddled together, Sophie could see them having a bit of a discussion. She wondered what they were saying. They all sat in silence watching. Even Ben and Sam seemed to know they should just lie down and behave.

After a few long minutes, the bomb squad went back to their truck and the police officers walked over to Sophie and Tom.

'The bomb squad say thank you for being so sensible. You are safe here but can't come any closer. They are going to lift the grenade out with a robot and take it away in a bomb bin,' said one of the officers.

'A bomb bin, what's that?' asked Sophie.

'It's a bin they put unexploded bombs in and then detonate them. They don't think this grenade will explode but they're not taking any chances. Just in case it's unstable. Well done you two, a good job. If it isn't stable, we could have had a nasty accident at the beach.'

Sophie watched amazed as a small robot with a long metal arm with pincers on the front moved slowly along the beach. It looked like a film set not real life; she wished she had a camera.

Now at the hole, its arm stretched out and reached down into the hole. As the arm came back out of the hole, Sophie could see the metal ball in its hand.

'Wow!' she said. 'Is that what a grenade looks like? It doesn't seem very big.'

Slowly, the clever robot put the grenade into the bin. Then it turned round and moved back towards the bomb squad.

'That was so clever,' said Tom. 'All done by remote control, that's amazing!'

Just then, the bomb disposal officer sent another machine out to pick up the bin and put it in the truck.

Sophie noticed that a small crowd was now gathering at the café, keen to see what was happening on the beach. They all clapped as the doors of the van closed and the bomb disposal officer gave a little bow. Sophie laughed – it was just like the theatre.

'Well, that was not what we were expecting to do this morning,' said Dad, 'but we are all safe and that is good. Just as well Leuchars is so close or we might have waited for hours.'

The police officers were now untying the blue and white ribbons and opening the beach up again and the little crowd at the café were jumping down onto the beach to look at the hole.

'Time for an early lunch I think,' said Dad, 'and then we will come back down this afternoon. Let's go.' They jumped off the rocks and headed over to the path.

'Hello!' shouted one of the police officers, waving to them. They stopped and he ran over to them. 'There are some photographers and a local news crew waiting at the other side to see if they can speak to you two,' he said, looking at Tom and Sophie. 'You will be celebrities by tonight, if that's okay with you and your dads.'

Sophie and Tom laughed – they were

surprised to see the photographers and news crew. They had a big microphone and big cameras on their shoulders. They looked at their dads.

'Can I?' they said together.

'It's fine with me,' said Tom's dad.

'And it's fine with me too,' said Sophie's dad.

Their dads watched as the news people directed them.

'Over here please,' said one of the photographers and Sophie and Tom took Ben and Sam over to the hole. Lights flashed. 'Can you look into the hole,' said another photographer. Sophie was feeling a bit shy; she noticed that the crowd on the beach were all interested in what was happening. Tom seemed to like having his photograph taken.

Then it was the local news team who had enormous furry mics. Tom explained about his school project and how he knew that it was possibly a grenade and he had called the police. Sophie explained that they were on holiday and came down to the beach most days with Sam and Ben who had been at puppy classes together.

'That was an exciting morning,' said Tom's dad as they walked back up the hill to the caravan park.

'I think we should all have tea at the café tonight and watch the news on the big TV screen – we might see some local celebrities,' said Dad, smiling. Tom's dad laughed as he put his arm around Tom.

'Good idea,' he said.

'See you later, Tom,' said Sophie, feeling happy now that all the excitement was over. She was impressed that Tom knew about World War 2; she wouldn't have known what to do.

After lunch, the whole family finally got to enjoy their quiet time on the beach, now that it was open again. Sophie reached into her beach bag and pulled out a towel and her new book. Harry and Max were really annoyed at missing the bomb squad and the robot and were busy playing with Sam and digging holes in case they found any more grenades! She smiled as she lay on her towel – hole number four was in the process of being dug, although Sophie thought it unlikely, they would find any more.

That night as they entered the café for tea, Sophie could see Tom and his mum and dad sitting at a long table near the TV.

'Special seats for special guests tonight,' said Carlos, the café owner. 'And free ice creams for both families – and our hero dogs of course!' Sam and Ben had been allowed into the café tonight as a reward for being clever; normally they had to sit at the outside tables. Sophie still felt it was like being in a theatre, it all felt quite unreal, but the free ice creams sounded good.

Sophie sat next to Tom and listened as

Harry asked him a hundred questions about bombs. 'Have you seen a bomb before? What colour was it? How big was it? Did you hear it explode?' Tom never got bored and answered all his questions.

Pizza was the choice tonight and some bowls of chips arrived too. Just as everyone started to tuck into their pizza, the news started and Sophie, Tom, Ben and Sam came onto the screen. Everyone in the restaurant cheered. Sophie reached down and gave Sam a wee cuddle, hiding her face in his soft fur. She noticed that Tom was smiling and she wished she was more confident. The news story looked good and she was pleased if a bit shy at what she said.

'Great to have celebs in tonight,' said the manager as he winked at Sophie and Tom.

Tummies full, they all headed back to the caravans.

'Bye Tom, Bye Ben,' said Sophie as she

cuddled Ben. 'We'll see you in the park.'

'Bye,' shouted Tom and his family as they headed into their caravan.

'That was an exciting end to the holiday,' said Mum giving Sophie a hug. 'Well done you.'

What a holiday, thought Sophie as she put her pyjamas on. She hadn't expected to find a grenade and be on the news; she wondered if any of her friends had watched her on TV!

Chapter 16
Where Is Gran?

'Sophie, Harry, are you dressed? It's just five minutes until I go to work,' Mum shouted upstairs. Reluctantly, Sophie pushed back her duvet; she had been having a lovely dream about playing with Sam on the beach at St Andrews.

As she was pulling on her clothes, Sophie heard Max opening the door to Gran and Grandpa. She headed down the stairs. 'Hi Gran, hi Grandpa,' she said, hugging them both.

'Hello Sophie, how did you and Sam get on at St Andrews?' asked Grandpa, winking at Gran.

'We had a lovely time. Did you see us on TV?' she asked.

Grandpa laughed. 'I certainly did! I saw Tom and Ben too. Do Gran and I have to curtsy and bow now that we are in the presence of a celebrity?'

'Haha, Grandpa,' said Sophie.

'It must have been a nice surprise to bump into Tom and Ben, your co-celebrities,' said Grandpa.

'Yea, they go every year. Tom loves it there like we do and he knows all the best places too. Sam and Ben were really good friends and they both loved the beach.'

'Great! And what are you up to today?' asked Grandpa.

'Is your nice friend Emma coming over to bake?' asked Gran.

'Yes, she's coming after breakfast.'

'Good, let's have breakfast now. What does everyone want?' asked Gran.

'Max, Harry and I are going to the park with Sam so porridge would be really good for us,' said Grandpa.

'Porridge for you too, Sophie?' asked Gran.

'Hmm, okay,' said Sophie, taking out the bowls and cutlery. 'I'll wash some berries for the porridge topping.

'Grandpa, do you want the telly on?' asked Harry.

'You are such good helpers,' said Gran as she stirred the porridge.

As she was finishing her porridge, Sophie heard Sam bark his usual 'hello' bark and realised Emma must have arrived.

'Hi Sophie, hi Gran,' shouted Emma as she walked through, stopping to tickle Sam's ears. 'You're such a lovely boy, Sam.'

'It's good that the boys and Grandpa are going to the park. We'll have peace to bake and chat,' said Gran.

'It's chocolate muffins today,' Sophie said to Emma.

'I love chocolate muffins,' said Emma. 'And I love mini Smartie toppings.' Sophie saw that Gran was listening, but she didn't say anything. Sophie waved goodbye to the boys.

'Right girls, let's get out the butter, sugar, eggs and scales,' said Gran, taking the flour out of the cupboard.

'Will I put the oven on to heat up?' asked Sophie.

'Good idea,' said Gran.

Sophie and Emma worked beside Gran, weighing and mixing, before eventually putting the mixture into twenty-four muffin cases. As she put the trays in the oven, Sophie noticed that Gran was hobbling a bit.

'Coffee time, Gran,' said Sophie, putting on the kettle.

'Thanks Sophie. The muffins are starting to smell delicious,' said Gran. 'Once they are baked, we will make the icing and then we can decorate them. I'm sure there will be some spare for your brothers Emma.'

'Thanks, they love it when I come to bake with Sophie,' said Emma.

The timer on the oven pinged and Emma and Sophie got up to take the muffins out. As the oven door opened, the smell of baked muffins drifted all around the kitchen; it was making Sophie feel quite hungry.

'Oh girls, I've forgotten to bring my toppings for the muffins. Could you go to the shop and buy some for me please? My old knees are a bit sore today and it saves me going on my scooter,' said Gran.

'No problem, we won't be long,' said Emma. Sophie wondered if Gran didn't have Emma's favourite mini smarties; she was sure Gran had heard her earlier.

They walked quickly to the shop, it was just a few streets away. It had a good selection of toppings and Gran had said to buy two, so they chose Emma's favourite, mini Smarties, and also some fudge cubes which were Grandpa's favourite.

As Emma and Sophie opened the front door, Sam ran to meet them. The boys and Grandpa were back. 'Hi Grandpa, did Sam behave?' asked Sophie.

'Good as gold, even when Max had the lead,' said Grandpa smiling. 'Is Gran with you?' he asked.

'No, we left her here, she asked us to go to the shop to buy two toppings. I made her a coffee to have while we were gone,' said Sophie.

'She went out when we came back, something about running out of ingredients and catching you at the shop,' said Grandpa.

'We didn't see her at the shop or on the way back. Is she on her scooter?' Sophie asked.

'Yes, she took her scooter; the shop is too far for her sore knees and she tells me her scooter is more eco-friendly than my car,' said Grandpa. 'Strange you didn't meet her.'

'Maybe she met one of her friends and is

having a chat,' said Sophie. 'Will Emma and I make lunch and we can decorate the muffins when Gran comes back?'

'That'll be perfect love, sandwiches will be just fine,' said Grandpa.

Emma and Sophie started to make a big plate of sandwiches, some cheese, some ham, some corned beef and some tomato for Gran. Harry put out plates, while Max filled a jug of orange juice and made a pot of tea for Gran and Grandpa.

'Lunch is ready,' shouted Sophie. 'Cakes later, when Gran comes back,' she said to Max who was just picking one up.

'Aw, not even one Sophie? You can't expect us to smell them and not eat them,' complained Harry.

'Okay, just one,' she said as they sat down. Harry and Max grabbed one each and started munching.

'Yum, good cakes Sophie,' said Harry.

It felt a bit strange having lunch with only Grandpa, but Sophie didn't say that. Grandpa looked a bit worried.

Sophie put Gran's tomato sandwiches on a plate and covered them; she would be hungry when she got back.

'I think I'm going to drive to the shop and just check Gran's scooter hasn't run out of battery. I'll take Max and Harry with me. Will you and Emma be okay? I won't be long. I don't want to leave the house empty in case Gran's back before me,' said Grandpa.

'No problem, Grandpa. She might be talking to Agnes, she lives not far from the shop,' said Sophie.

'I'll check with Agnes if we haven't met her first,' said Grandpa.

Sophie and Emma were tidying up the kitchen when the phone rang. 'Hello,' said Sophie.

'Oh, hello Mum... Grandpa has gone out to look for Gran, he thinks her scooter might have run out of battery... Okay, I'll tell him. Bye Mum.'

As Sophie hung up the phone, she heard the front door open and ran through to see Grandpa, Max and Harry coming in. 'Did you find Gran?'

'No love, I didn't. She isn't back then?' said Grandpa. 'Dave at the shop hasn't seen her and neither has Agnes. Where can she be?' he said, puzzled.

'Mum called, she said if you didn't find her you should call Dad, he is at a meeting quite nearby,' said Sophie.

'Good idea, I'll give him a call now. I'm getting a bit concerned – she has been away for two hours now and that isn't like her,' said Grandpa.

Sophie and Emma sat at the kitchen table watching the clock hands which now said half past one.

Sophie jumped up when she heard the front door opening again.

'Hello,' said Dad as he came into the kitchen. 'I hear Gran's gone out for some shopping and isn't back yet.' She could see Dad giving Grandpa a puzzled look.

'I drove round the usual streets, but I couldn't see her or her scooter,' said Grandpa.

'Well, we'll check some other streets just in case she took a different route,' said Dad.

Just as they were discussing who was going and who was staying in case Gran came back, the front doorbell rang. They all rushed through.

It was Emma's mum. 'Emma called me. I hear Gran hasn't returned from her shopping. I can stay and look after Max and Harry if that helps while you look.'

'That is really kind, thank you,' said Dad, catching his jacket from the hall hook just as

Grandpa pulled on his coat. Emma and Sophie climbed into the back seat of the car.

'I'll drive slowly,' said Dad.

Twice they drove round all the streets, up and down and across. Where could she be wondered Sophie.

'Okay, let's go home, Gran might be back,' said Dad.

Sophie ran in but Gran wasn't there. Dad and Grandpa were now both looking really concerned.

'I think I'll ask Andrew for some advice,' said Dad. 'He will be happy to help.' Andrew was a local police officer and he was very friendly; he liked Sam and always stopped to give him a pat when he passed.

'I think that's a good idea,' said Grandpa. Dad left and returned a little later with Andrew. Emma and her mum were still there, playing with Max and Harry. The chocolate muffins were still on the cooling rack in the kitchen, waiting to be decorated. No-one had asked to eat any more.

'I think we need to search a little bit wider now. It seems as if you have checked all the streets to the shops thoroughly,' said Andrew.

'We'll drive a few streets further out and then walk in pairs and stay in contact.'

'Dad, do you think we should take Sam?' asked Sophie. 'He might be a help if we are walking.'

'That's a good idea. Gran's scarf is in the kitchen, we'll take that with us for Sam to smell,' said Dad.

They drove some extra streets and parked the car. 'Sam, come and smell this, see if you can find Gran,' Sophie said, putting the scarf out for him to smell. Sam did as he was told. They looked up and down all the driveways but there was no sign of Gran's red scooter or Gran. Sam didn't seem to smell anything.

Just as they were walking past the lane towards the farm, Sam suddenly started to pull on the lead. 'Sam, where are you going?' asked Sophie. She took the scarf out of her pocket. 'Sam, smell this, we're looking for Gran,' she said. Sam kept pulling her towards the path.

'Let's follow him,' said Dad. 'We can't see Gran, so it is worth a look.'

They followed Sam whose nose was now on the ground. He was moving quickly, smelling the middle of the path. Sophie kept the scarf in her hand and let Sam smell it as they moved forward. At the end of the path, the walkers' gate was open and Sam pulled them into the field; he barked then stopped and barked again.

'He smells something,' said Sophie, letting him off his lead. Sam ran straight across the field to the far corner. Sophie and Dad ran after him trying their best to keep up with him and, as they got closer, they saw Gran's red scooter, beside a bush. Sam was now running round it and Gran was sitting on it, waving.

'Oh, I'm so glad you found me, I didn't know how to get back home,' said Gran. 'I was a bit worried.'

Sophie thought she looked cold and very pale. 'Gran, we were so worried about you,' she said, giving her a great big hug.

'Thank goodness,' said Dad as he called Andrew. 'Mission accomplished, an old lady and her scooter found,' said Dad, grinning at Gran. Sophie heard him give directions and in a few minutes, Sophie saw Grandpa and Andrew running across the field.

Out of breath, Grandpa said, 'Are you okay, I was so worried. How did you get here?'

'Well before the explanations, I think I'm going to call for an ambulance. Gran looks a bit pale and exhausted. I think a doctor needs to check her over,' said Andrew.

'Good idea,' said Dad pulling out his phone.

'Oh, what a fuss. I was just a bit silly. I wanted to pop in and see Jean and I thought it might be quicker to go across the fields but then my scooter got stuck. I definitely don't need an ambulance, just a nice cup of tea will be fine,' said Gran.

'Okay, but if the cup of tea doesn't make you feel better, then Andrew is right, you need to see a doctor. I will bring the car up to the edge of the field and Grandpa and Sophie will help you to the car,' said Dad.

'I'll ask Jim if he can pull your scooter out with his tractor,' said Andrew. He had tried to start it but Gran was right – it was really stuck in the mud.

'Thanks Andrew, tell him I'm sorry to cause him extra work.'

Dad wasn't long in bringing the car over

and Sophie was pleased to see that Gran managed to walk to the car without much help and they all piled in. Gran waved to Andrew as they drove away.

Mum opened the front door as they arrived home. 'Hello, it's so good to see you are okay,' she said, giving Gran a hug. 'Sit down on a comfy seat and I'll make you a cup of tea.'

'I'm so sorry – did you come home from work early? And Emma's mum is here too. I really did a very silly thing taking my scooter across the field, I won't do it again. I didn't mean to worry anyone,' said Gran.

'That's good news,' said Dad who was smiling now as Mum brought a tray of hot drinks through. 'Just as well we have Sam, he was such a big help. It would have been much harder to find you without him.'

Sophie smiled – Gran was okay and Dad was glad to have Sam. Sam was doing a good job of training Dad. He was a clever puppy. It wasn't such a bad day after all.

'Thank you, Sam! I love you, you are a really special dog,' said Gran. Grandpa nodded. Poor Grandpa thought Sophie, he had had a big fright too. Sophie noticed Sam was lying in between both their feet. What a caring puppy he is she thought.

'This tea is lovely and I am enjoying the shortbread, but Sophie – where are the muffins?' asked Gran.

'We waited for you to come back before we finished them,' said Sophie.

'Well, I'm back now. The icing is in a piping bag in the fridge. You and Emma can decorate the cakes while I drink this nice tea. Then Emma can take some home,' said Gran.

Sophie smiled, 'Come on Emma, we better get icing these cakes,' she said as she stood up. She was pleased to see that Gran seemed to be back to her old self. As she walked past the window, Sophie noticed flashing lights and a large tractor at the end of the driveway. 'Gran, I think Jim has brought your scooter back,' she said.

'Oh, he is kind. What a lot of trouble I have been today. Getting stuck on my scooter was not my best idea I'm such an old nuisance,' said Gran.

'You are not an old nuisance Gran,' said Harry, jumping up and giving her a hug. 'It's okay to make mistakes, I do it all the time.' Everyone laughed.

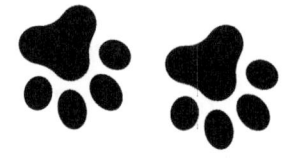

Chapter 17
Birthday Surprises

Sophie opened her eyes and wondered what surprises might be in store today for her birthday. She already had a wonderful puppy, who had found Gran last week. She got dressed quickly and ran down the stairs and into the kitchen.

'Happy birthday Sophie!' said Mum.

'Happy birthday, grown-up girl! Eleven already,' said Dad, hugging her.

'I don't think I feel any different to ten yet,' laughed Sophie.

'This is one of your presents, we've another one for you later when Gran and Grandpa are here,' said Mum. Sophie hugged her mum as she took the large parcel, prettily wrapped with a purple ribbon and large sparkly bow. She wondered what could possibly be in such a large box.

'My favourite colour,' said Sophie, peeling

the ribbon off. Inside the large box was a big empty space and a little wrapped box at the bottom. 'This is starting to feel like Christmas,' said Sophie. 'But no note this time, just a little parcel.' Mum and Dad laughed.

Sophie pulled the next wrapper off and inside was a long blue box. McKay was written on it in silver letters and Sophie smiled – it was the jewellery shop in the village. She often stopped to look in the window. She opened the lid and inside was a beautiful silver bracelet shining on the dark blue velvet lining.

'Thank you, thank you,' she said, hugging Mum and Dad. 'It's amazing, some of the other girls have bracelets like this and I love them.'

'We know. Have you checked the charms?' asked Mum.

'Oh, it's a dog and a snowman!' said Sophie. 'They're perfect.'

Just then she heard Max and Harry singing

loudly, 'Happy birthday to you, happy birthday to you,' as they carried a parcel between them. Sophie laughed.

'Thank you,' she said, taking the parcel and hugging her brothers.

'I wrapped it,' said Harry.

'I'd never have guessed,' said Sophie, looking at all the sticky tape Harry had wound round the parcel. She tugged and pulled at the wrapping and Harry and Max laughed as she struggled to open it. But with a big tug, the parcel finally split open and her favourite chocolate buttons fell out, along with a book and a bag of dog treats.

'I chose the book,' said Max.

'And I chose the buttons for you and the treats for Sam,' said Harry.

'I love it all, thank you,' said Sophie.

'Gran and Grandpa are coming to the restaurant with us for tea tonight. How many friends did you invite?'

'Just five, Emma, Hannah, Jodie, Fatima and Anna,' said Sophie.

'Great, I'll let the restaurant know. And now we need to get ready for school and work,' said Dad, picking up the breakfast dishes.

Sophie went to collect Sam for his walk and smiled as she saw an envelope in his bed. It had 'Sophie' written on it. She opened the envelope; there was a paw print on the card inside. 'Thank you, Sam,' she said, hugging him. Sophie saw Mum smile at Dad.

'Hi Sophie, happy birthday,' said Victoria as they all headed to school.

'Thanks Victoria,' said Sophie, taking a card from her. 'Oh, one with a dog, that's lovely.'

She watched as they entered the black metal school gates. Victoria ran into the playground with Harry and joined a group of girls who waved and shouted to her. Sophie smiled – all seemed well, even though she had moved on to Primary Three.

'Hi Sophie, happy birthday,' shouted Emma and Fatima. Sophie went to join her own friends. Right after register, the class sang happy birthday to her and she chose one of the birthday cards from the box. They all made cards at the start of the year and when it was your birthday, you got to choose one. As she opened it, she saw a big bunch of colourful balloons on the front and that Karim had signed the artwork. 'Thanks Karim,' she said, 'it's really good.'

It had been a good day at school. Primary Seven had been good so far. Mrs Carmichael was different to Mrs Johnstone but she was a nice teacher too, quite strict but kind and always fair.

As they were all heading home, her friends chatted about their outfits for tonight. Anna and Fatima were having her nails painted and sparkly diamantes placed on top.

Sophie was pleased she had chosen a restaurant dinner and not a party.

'See you later, Soph,' the girls called as she turned onto her street.

She could see Gran and Grandpa's car outside the house. She hadn't seen them since Gran's scooter in the field day. She was hoping Grandpa would come for a walk with her and Sam before they went to the restaurant – Sam always seemed to want to show Grandpa his best behaviour. He didn't chase rabbits or ducks at the park when Grandpa was there.

'Hi Gran, hi Grandpa,' she said, running in and giving them a hug.

'Hello birthday girl,' said Grandpa.

'Happy birthday, Sophie,' said Gran, handing her a parcel. Sophie noticed that Sam was lying at Gran's feet, well actually more on her feet. 'He has been keeping an eye on me,' said Gran, laughing.

'We'll all be keeping an eye on you!' said Grandpa.

Sophie opened her parcel; it was another box which said McKay on it. 'Wow, more jewellery,' said Sophie.

'Well, you look in that window every time we pass,' laughed Grandpa.

Sophie opened the box and inside on the blue velvet lining was a pretty necklace with a silver heart. Her name was engraved on the front and when she turned it over, Sam's name was engraved on the back. 'It's really special, thank you,' she said, hugging them both.

'Well, I'm very glad that you and Sam found me. You're a special pair,' said Gran.

'They certainly are,' said Dad. 'That's a lovely necklace, Sophie.'

'Maybe you and Grandpa can take Sam for a walk while Gran has a cup of tea,' said Mum.

'And then when you get home, you can change for

the restaurant.'

'Okay, we'll just have a short walk,' said Sophie.

It wasn't too long before Sophie and Grandpa returned. Sophie fed Sam and then ran upstairs to choose an outfit for her birthday tea. She was really looking forward to it. She felt at eleven that she didn't want a party with games.

As she was trying to choose her outfit, she heard a knock at the door and Sam barked to say 'hello'.

'Sophie, can you come down please, there are two visitors to see you,' shouted Dad.

'Just coming,' Sophie shouted back, wondering who had come to see her as she ran down the stairs. Harry and Max were running down behind her.

Sophie was surprised to see Andrew, the policeman who had helped find Gran, and another police officer who had gold braids on her shoulders and her hat.

'Hello Sophie,' said Andrew, sitting down on the couch. 'This is Inspector McMurdo and she would like to speak to you about Sam.'

'About Sam?' she said, feeling puzzled.

'Yes Sophie, PC McMillan here was telling me how helpful Sam was in finding Gran,' said Inspector McMurdo.

'Yes, he seemed able to smell her from her scarf.'

'I also hear that it isn't the first time Sam has helped someone,' said Inspector McMurdo. 'So, we would like to give him a special award to say thank you for helping others.'

'An award?' she said in surprise. 'An award, Sam – just for you! Thank you,' she said as she tickled his ears. He wasn't one yet and he had already won an award – wow, thought Sophie.

'That is a very special honour for Sam and

Sophie,' said Dad. 'Thank you, Inspector McMurdo.'

'You're very welcome, we're pleased to be able to give Sam an award. Sophie, you'll receive a letter which will tell you the date, time and place of the award ceremony. And if it is okay, we would like to take a photograph of you and Sam at the ceremony.'

'That's okay,' said Sophie. She couldn't quite believe this was all happening, and on her birthday.

'There is just one other thing we would like to ask,' said Inspector McMurdo. 'Do you think you would consider allowing us to train Sam to find people? He seems to be very good at it.'

'What does that involve?' asked Dad.

'Well, we would only use him locally, so Andrew here would do the special dog training with him which would take a few weeks and then he would borrow him when we had a local missing person,' said Inspector McMurdo. 'But you don't have to decide today. Talk to Andrew over the next week and you can let me know at the award ceremony.'

'Does Sam have to go far away for the training?' asked Sophie.

'No, it's all done locally and we can do it while you are at school – he would be home by teatime,' said Andrew. 'But we'll go now and let you enjoy your party. Don't worry about it Sophie, we'll chat next week,' said Andrew.

Dad showed Inspector McMurdo and Andrew out. 'Don't worry Sophie, he's your dog and we won't agree to anything you're not happy about,' said Dad, giving Sophie a hug. Sophie nodded and knelt beside Sam who rolled over to have his tummy tickled.

'Sam, I love you, you're a clever dog, and you're mine, you'll always be mine,' said Sophie, hugging him. Brightening up she said, 'You'll need a haircut and a bath before the award ceremony, your photo is going to be in the newspaper.'

Sophie headed back upstairs and chose her best jeans, some sparkly sandals and the new white top Gran had brought her back from a shopping trip with Mum. She carefully put on her new necklace and bracelet and brushed her hair. When she looked in the mirror, she felt quite grown up. Maybe eleven was more grown up than ten, she thought as she headed back down the stairs. 'Looking lovely Sophie and definitely eleven,' said Dad giving her a hug.

'Okay, let's go. I'm starving. Mum and I have that other parcel, but we'll give it to you after the restaurant, it'll need a bit of time.'

Sophie wondered what kind of present needed time. She gave Sam a wee treat and a hug as they were leaving, 'See you later Sam, be good.' Sam took his treat to his bed and lay down. Sophie felt sad she was leaving him behind.

As she entered the restaurant, she looked at the mixture of purple and white balloons on the very long table, with one which said 'Happy Birthday' in the middle. Sophie felt very special as she sat down with her family. Within a few minutes, her friends all appeared with gifts and more balloons. This was an amazing birthday. Everyone settled and the whole table seemed to be enjoying the treat – even her brothers were smiling at one another.

Several large pizzas and some bowls of pasta, garlic bread and salad all arrived. It was quite a feast, spread out along the tabletop. Everyone tucked in and it didn't take long for the food to disappear.

'Puddings anyone?' asked Dad when the last of the dinner plates had been cleared. He nodded to the waiter who took the orders. Sophie wasn't sure whether to have ice cream or a fudge Brownie, but the waiter winked and said that birthday girls could have both.

'This ice cream is yummy,' Sophie heard Harry say to Fatima.

'Mine is even better than yours,' said Max, stealing a spoonful of Harry's.

Just as Harry was about to complain, the table was suddenly surrounded by staff making an enormous noise, banging pots and pans and singing 'Happy Birthday' as everyone in the restaurant joined in. Sophie felt her face go pink. She saw one waiter carrying the biggest chocolate cake ever with purple candles glowing all around the edge. As the waiter put the cake in front of Sophie and the singing stopped, she took a deep breath and blew the candles out; she closed her eyes and made a wish while everyone cheered. She really hoped her wish would come true.

No-one, not even Max or Harry, had space for the chocolate cake. 'I think we will just take the cake home, and perhaps Sophie's friends could have a slice to take home too,' Dad said to the waiter.

'No problem,' said the waiter and the girls each received a white box with a large slice of cake inside. Sophie gave her friends a little party bag each with a nail polish, a lip balm, some nice chocolate and a bath bomb to thank them for coming to her birthday dinner.

'Thanks Sophie, see you tomorrow at school,' they shouted as their parents picked them up.

Back home and with the large cake box safely on the table, Dad said, 'That was a fantastic evening Sophie, a good choice. And now your last parcel, and I have one for Gran too.'

'A parcel for me?' said Gran. 'It isn't my birthday.'

'I know but this is important,' said Dad. 'You should both open at the same time. Ready, steady, go,' he said as he handed out the parcels.

Harry and Max looked on as Sophie and Gran tore open their identical presents. Grandpa laughed as Sam tried to help Sophie, tugging at one end. He loved parcels.

'A mobile! Thank you, thank you – lots of my friends have one now,' said Sophie.

'Oh, I'm not sure,' said Gran.

'It's a matter of safety, we're never going to have a losing Gran situation again,' said Dad. 'Now you can call for help if you need it.'

'If you give it to me, Gran, I can show you what to do,' said Max.

'I was going to buy Gran one myself, it's a great idea,' said Grandpa.

'I suppose you're right,' said Gran, giving the phone to Max.

'I think after all this excitement, it's time I took Gran home. It's been a lovely evening, a proper grown-up party for a grown-up granddaughter,' said Grandpa, hugging Sophie.

That night in bed, Sophie thought about all the nice surprises she'd had on her eleventh birthday. It had been a very special day – an award for Sam, a restaurant party, new jewellery and now a mobile phone too. And an award ceremony in the village hall to look forward to, clever Sam. Eleven, it seems, is quite different to ten. But sharing Sam with the police – she wasn't so sure about that, he was her puppy.

Chapter 18
A Special Award

It was strange – she was eleven years old and Sam was now eleven months old, his first birthday was next month, in October.

Although Sam was naughty sometimes, he really was an amazing puppy and definitely knew when someone needed help. Sophie had no idea how he knew, he just seemed to have some sort of talent. He had found Mark at the beach and had found Gran when she went missing, and he had noticed when Colin and Victoria were upset. That was a lot of helping for a small puppy. He also helped Mum pull the washing out of the washing machine all the time, that was funny to watch. She had put a video on YouTube and he had two thousand followers, it was amazing. Oh, and he had helped himself to some biscuits, jumping up onto the table for them – but that was a very different kind of helping and certainly not one he would win awards for! Dad had not been pleased. Harry and Max thought it was hilarious but Dad just gave them a row too.

Her teacher Mrs Carmichael was pleased to hear about Sam's award. At lunchtime, Sophie found Mrs Johnstone, her teacher from Primary Six, and she was delighted to hear about Sam's award too.

'I knew from the day you brought him into school that he really responded well to the children. He is certainly special, well done,' she said.

Mrs Hamilton told the whole school about the award at assembly that week. Sophie went out to the front of the assembly to explain to all the classes why Sam was being given an award and all the children clapped. Sophie felt her face go pink again.

After assembly, Mrs Hamilton asked her to come to her office. Sophie knocked on her door, even though it was open.

'Ah, hello Sophie, I just wanted to say that it is wonderful news about Sam. You must be feeling very proud of him, and we are very proud of you. Mrs Johnstone was telling me how well you look after him. Your dad sent me an email to ask if you could have the afternoon off school for the award ceremony and of course you can. But I have a dog too and I know that they are part of the family so I think Max and Harry should go too. I'll suggest it to your dad.'

'Thank you Mrs Hamilton,' Sophie beamed.

Wow, she thought as she walked back to class, Harry and Max will be delighted.

'Really Sophie, we can go too?' said Max.

Harry ran round them shouting:

'Cool, cool

to be off school,

that's my new poem!'

Sophie laughed.

A few days later, Sophie and Mum took Sam to the dog grooming salon – it was his first puppy haircut.

'Hi, I'm Jenny and I will be his groomer today,' said a young woman as Sophie handed her Sam's lead. Sam looked back, wondering if Sophie was coming too, then he trotted off with Jenny. They sat in the waiting room and chatted about the award ceremony. Sophie laughed when he came back.

'Oh, look at you – you're all smooth,' said Sophie, running her hand along his glossy coat. Jenny held out a basket of bows for Sophie to choose one for Sam and she chose red.

'His curls will grow back, Sophie,' said Jenny as she handed him back.

'Thanks, he is a very smart boy,' said Mum as they left.

'Who is this dog?' said Harry, pretending

not to recognise Sam as he came into the lounge and Sam ran through his legs and barked. 'Oh, it's you Sam,' he said laughing as he lay on the floor and tickled Sam's tummy.

Chapter 19
A Special Day

Sophie met Harry and Max at the school gates and they rushed home – it was Sam's big day.

'Do you know what happens, Sophie?' asked Max. 'Will he get a big medal or a trophy?'

'I'm not sure, we just need to wait and see.'

Dad's car was already in the driveway; it was a big day for everyone.

'Do I really have to wear my school uniform?' asked Harry as he munched on his cheese roll.

'Yes, you'll look very smart,' said Mum.

Harry knew that was the end of the discussion and didn't complain anymore.

'I'll walk Sam, Sophie, you go and get ready.' said Dad.

Sophie was feeling very excited about the award ceremony. She went upstairs to put on her new dress and her birthday necklace and bracelet. She brushed her hair and tied it up in a ponytail with a red ribbon – she wanted to match Sam. They were a team.

When they arrived at the village hall, it was quite busy.

'Relatives on these rows please,' said a man in a smart uniform who directed Mum, Dad, Gran, Grandpa, Harry and Max into rows in the middle of the hall. 'Award winners on the front row please, the seats have your names on them.'

Sophie found her name and sat down with Sam at her feet. She turned to wave and Gran and Grandpa waved back. On her left was a fireman.

'Hello,' he said. 'I like your dog. What's his name?'

'Sam,' replied Sophie just as some music started to play and the hall fell silent.

The Mayor, walking very tall, came into the room; in front of her were two men wearing suits. Behind her were Inspector McMurdo and a lady in a fire service uniform. Sophie thought that the Mayor's large chains, which hung round her neck, looked very heavy. The group of important-looking people all sat down on some great big wooden carved chairs behind a long wooden table, except for the Mayor who stood.

'Good afternoon and welcome to our award ceremony. Today, we have six very special guests who have helped others and our village is very proud to make these awards to them today,' said the Mayor.

The fireman, who was called John, was called first – he had saved three children from a house fire. Next, Sophie heard Sam's name. She stood up and said 'let's go' to Sam as they walked forward. The Mayor put a large medal on a ribbon round Sam's neck and as they walked back to their seat, Sophie could see her family all clapping and waving. It was amazing.

She was pleased that the ceremony didn't

last too long, it wasn't easy to keep Sam sitting still. The photographer took several photographs of Sam by himself and some of them both. He was popular, with everyone coming to talk to him; he loved the attention, he looked like a dog born for the stage, enjoying all the fuss.

After the photographs, Grandpa treated them all to tea at a local hotel. He had booked a small room just for them so that Sam could come too. This time there was a round table with a white tablecloth set out for eight. Just as Sophie was wondering why eight, Aunty Claire popped her head round the door.

'Surprise!' she said. 'I couldn't miss Sam's big day.' Sam ran straight over and gave his usual one bark before running round her legs, sitting on her feet and rolling over onto his back, waiting for her to tickle his tummy. 'You are so gorgeous,' she said as she tickled him.

Grandpa had ordered big bowls of lentil soup, then steak pie and of course chocolate cake and ice cream for pudding. Sam had a plate of steak pie without the pastry, which he loved.

'That was delicious,' said Dad. 'Thank you for such a lovely treat.'

'Thanks Grandpa,' said Sophie, Max and

Harry, taking their cue from Dad.

It was a special day thought Sophie as she put Sam's medal in her jewellery box, a day she knew she would remember forever.

That night, as she stood in the back garden with Sam, she looked at the dark sky, stars twinkling on their black canvas. When Sam had arrived on Christmas morning ten months ago, she had been worried that Dad might not like him; she didn't need to worry about that anymore – she knew Dad loved him, she could tell by the way he spoke to him.

She had hoped that she would be good at looking after Sam and she had a Bronze Award to say she was, with Silver puppy training starting after Christmas this year.

Her puppy was becoming a very special dog not only to her but to other people too. Maybe he would find someone who needed help someday then perhaps sharing him a little would be the right thing to do. For now she would just think about it.

He was such a special part of the family now too. Harry and Max might tease him at times, and sometimes Sam teased them, stealing their balls or books and running away with them and of course a chasing game began.

Her wish had come true and was better than she had ever imagined.

'Sophie, what are you doing out here?' said Mum.

'I'm just watching Sam,' said Sophie.

'He is such a special boy; I can't remember how life was without him. Oh, look at that lovely shooting star over there.'

Sophie watched its trail fade as it moved across the sky. She closed her eyes.

Smiling, she wondered if it would come true by the time she was twelve.

Puppy Quiz for New Owners

True or False

1. Dogs need: food, water and a bed.
2. Chew toys help puppies stop biting/ chewing on your things.
3. A puppy needs a bath every day.
4. A puppy needs to build up the length of its walks to protect its joints.
5. It is okay for your puppy to help itself to food on your plate.
6. Puppies are always naughty.
7. You should train your puppy to sit before it crosses a road.
8. To be a good puppy owner you need to be; loving, fun and firm.

Answers to Puppy Quiz

1. True
2. True
3. False, puppies less than eight weeks shouldn't have a bath and after that usually once a month is enough.
4. True, walks start at ten minutes and build up over several months.
5. False, you don't want your dog to steal food that might be bad for them.
6. False, you can teach them good behaviours.
7. True, it is good to be safe.
8. True, puppies need kind responsible owners.

Acknowledgements

I loved writing *Sam the Superstar Puppy*, it was both a pleasure and hard work. During this journey of creativity, I was grateful for the support and encouragement I received from a variety of colleagues, friends and family. Thank you to Nikki, Lyndsay and Karen who read early edits. I am grateful to editors, Becky and Fiona who challenged my flow and offered wise counsel as I drew closer to final drafts and to Mandy for beautiful artwork. To Myra my heartfelt thanks for your encouragement and belief in my work. Thank you to all my friends and family who asked about my progress and encouraged me to keep writing.

Printed in Great Britain
by Amazon